Reviews from the Authonomy Community:

'I finished KILL ALL MEN today, and it's hands down the funniest thing I've ever read.. It will be hard to find a publisher because [it] pokes at Muslims, sluts, marriage, fidelity, cat people, women, government, the educational system, foreigners, sex, gays, alpha and beta males, and children. Great job. There's no one left to alienate.. This certainly won't appeal to everyone, but lots of readers are craving stuff like [this].'
- Digsblues – Top 500 Amazon Reviewer (USA)

'I've read the hype about this book and it's worth checking out. Satirical, true to the context.. Good job! High stars!'
- Johan Bordones - Author of 'Cate'

'Perfect. Probably some professional posing as a "newbie".. GREAT, great voice.'
- Patrick Ross - Author of 'Three Men on a Bender'

'Excellent comedy.. Anyone looking for something humorous (but of substance) should read [this] book.. All 6 stars.'
- Aminul Ruhul Islam - Author of 'Agent of Allah'

'For a work of comedy it is flawless. I think everyone who works in the public sector (which I did briefly and f****** hated it) or hates their job should read this.'
- Joe Carter - Author of 'The Corruption of Michael Blake'

'I loved this. [The] MC is so crude and narcissistic, and his superior intelligence should make him unbearable but it doesn't. The fact that he rages against everything in equal measure takes the sharp edge off the rants and makes them comic. I find his dry understanding of the world very funny indeed, and that self-awareness is great.. High stars.'
- Andy Paine - Author of 'Bad Business' and 'The Life and Lies of Danny Diaz'

Kill All Men

Phil Hipside

Disclaimer

All characters appearing in this work are fictitious. The views, opinions and positions expressed by the characters in this book do not necessarily reflect the views, opinions or positions of the author or anyone he knows. Names, characters, businesses, places, events and incidents are either the products of the author's imagination or used in a fictitious manner. This is a work of parody and satire. Any quotations, transcripts, excerpts and song lyrics are used in a 'fair use' context but remain the copyright of their respective owners.

C'mon people, this is a work of fiction. If you need more help in discerning fiction from reality, I recommend seeing a good therapist. Any resemblance to real persons living or dead, or actual events is purely coincidental. Except you, Svetlana. You know what you did. Live with your shame - bitch.

Copyright © 2012 Phil Hipside
All rights reserved.
ISBN: 1499711190
ISBN-13: 978-1499711196

DEDICATION

Mam. Words would never do you justice. RIP

CONTENTS

Acknowledgments

1	Roles and Responsibilities	Pg 1
2	Boundaries	Pg 11
3	Induction, Icebreakers and Ground Rules	Pg 21
4	Codes of Practice	Pg 31
5	Teaching and Learning Environment	Pg 43
6	Learning Styles	Pg 51
7	Key Theories of Learning	Pg 66
8	Motivation	Pg 76
9	Needs of the Organisation	Pg 86
10	Initial, Diagnostic Assessment	Pg 98
11	Points of Referral	Pg 110
12	Equality and Diversity	Pg 121
13	Inclusive Learning	Pg 134
14	Schemes of Work and Session Plans	Pg 146
15	Differentiation	Pg 157
16	Resources	Pg 167
17	Literacy, Language and Numeracy	Pg 175
18	Information and Communication Technology	Pg 184
19	Record Keeping	Pg 198
20	Teaching and Learning Approaches	Pg 206
21	Communication, Behaviour and Respect	Pg 218
22	Working with Groups and Individuals	Pg 231
23	Safeguarding	Pg 242
24	Planning for Assessment	Pg 253
25	Assessment Types	Pg 263
26	Assessment Methods	Pg 285
27	Making Decisions and Giving Feedback	Pg 291

ABOUT THE AUTHOR   Pg 305

ACKNOWLEDGMENTS

Thanks to my family, for allowing me the time and space to write and being so wonderful.

Thanks to my writing group:

Jess Richards, author of 'Snake Ropes' and 'Cooking with Bones,' for setting the bar so high and being such an inspiration

Lucy Deslandes, for not understanding anything I write, but reading it anyway and never letting my wine glass go dry.

Dave Chowcat, for being so scrupulously honest and giving it to me straight.

Noel O'Reilly, for warning me about agents and the publishing industry - you were spot on.

Ericka Waller, author of 'Confessions of a Mother Inferior,' for giving me the kick up the arse that I really needed.

Thanks to the guys down the pub and on Authonomy, especially Dan, Mo and Digsblues for their proof reading efforts.

As a cash-strapped, indie author, publicity is a bit of a crowd sourcing, on going endeavour, so a big thanks to all those who are helping to spread the word.

1 ROLES AND RESPONSIBILITIES

I'm thinking:

'Give a man a fish and you feed him for a day. Teach a man to fish and with tuition fees, student loans and living expenses, you feed the financial sector for life.'

Granted it's a bit longwinded, but the deadline is today, and if a marketing master of the universe like myself doesn't win the college's motto competition, frankly it'll be a travesty.

Someone's been sending me flowers again. They're sat on my desk with no card. On the other side of the desk, twirling a strand of blonde hair around her index finger, one of my students - Casey, is harping on about some problem she's having with her degree project. I'm stood next to the office window, blowing smoke rings through the opening, deep in thought and watching some Asian kids - probably business students, walk through the car park stuffing egg McMuffins down their necks.

Others students lumber into the lobby. The wall next to

reception displays thought provoking but ultimately meaningless aphorisms promoting 'Women's Month.' Someone has spray-mounted images of Rosemary West and Myra Hindley over the faces. The month before that it was 'Black History Month' on which someone pasted Robert Mugabe and Idi Amin. Again, no one noticed. The month before, it was 'Disability' with Abu Hamza and Oscar Pistorius. Before that - who knows, 'Mongolian Bestiality Month' with - I don't know, Graham Norton or someone. And yet, not a single complaint crosses the desk of the Equality and Diversity officer.

Apathy is our youth's greatest attribute - you only have to take a quick glance around here to realise that. Great Britain - active war weary citizens to passive x-factor consumers within a few generations. Fighting against this immovable force is like the war on drugs or terror; it just can't be won. So we should embrace it, particularly as it is also our nation's most superabundant asset; our greatest defence against revolution and change. Exploited effectively it could conceivably form the basis of our economic future too. I should write to Simon Cowell with some ideas; a guy who really knows how to harness this sort of stuff but frankly, I can't be arsed.

The college day starts at 10am so the students can use off peak rail fares. The day finishes at 4pm for the same reason. An hour for lunch and twenty minutes either side for a tea break makes for a little over a four-hour day in which students habitually bitch about their workload to their online network - usually during study time. This is our future talent and tax-payers being primed for the globalised work place.

In China, kids do maths Olympics at weekends for fun. In South Korea they start the school day at 7am and get home at 11pm, then they're put through national service for good measure. It's taken them from illiterate backwater to economic powerhouse within two generations. Things can change that fast - either way. If the future economic prospects of a country are reliant on it's youth, then we are truly up shit creek. Get out while you can because in a few years we'll all be packing ourselves in freight containers and making for migration processing centres in the South China Sea.

Down the corridor I hear a door slam. I hear this because the office door is open. The office door is open because college code of practice decrees a tutor cannot have 'contact time' with a student behind a closed door.

Go figure.

College policy also decrees a tutor cannot call students, 'students'. It's pejorative. They're 'learners' in line with the Qualifications and Credit Framework (QCF). Education does so love its stupid bloody acronyms.

Wheezing through the doorway comes Henry. Henry has an inhaler permanently attached to his gob. I keep trying to get the nickname 'Steamboat Willie' to trend amongst the students, but it's just not catching on. Again apathy defeats me. Even with a 10am start he still can't drag himself in on time. The fact that this retard is several pay grades higher than me and my line manager makes me puke.

Yes, literally.

His forehead is beaded with sweat like some catholic priest at a kiddie pool. He flashes me a weary smile and wipes his face with a handkerchief.

The bullet points you should be making on Henry are these:

- He drives an eight-year old, purple, Peugeot 307.
- He has shoulder length greying hair and a beard to match.
- He's about 50, clinically obese and has high cholesterol.
- He's from the North.

What the hell can someone in that state teach kids anything about advertising and marketing; about adver-gaming, viral spamming or long tail trending? He hasn't worked in the industry in nearly two decades. He hasn't worked out - probably ever. In the public sector, where a diversity, inclusivity and equality obsession trumps any form of merit; where there are constant calls for staff to be more representative of the British population, I suppose the HR department have truly out done themselves by employing this particular specimen. I nod at him needlessly, as he dumps his bag at his desk and hurries back out for his first class then return my attention to blowing smoke rings out of the window and not listening to Casey.

Back in the car park, one of the students has spread his chips over the cashmere silver metallic paint job of my BMW to share with his mates.

'Casey?' I say, my jaw set so tight I can barely speak. Uncurling the blonde strand from her index finger she suddenly sits up like a meerkat.

'Mmm?'

'Go and tell those terrorists to get their chips off my car please.'

Jumping up and seeing the kids she stifles a giggle.

'You can't call them that Carl, it's racial,' she tells me.

'It's not 'racial,' Casey,' I tell her wisely. 'It's stereotyping. There's a difference.'

I offer her a drag of my smoke and she takes it. We're bonding. Sharing my fag, using my first name, she's telling me this: We're both adults. In education we call this 'instinctive learning.' She places a hand on my chest, letting it linger longer than strictly necessary and I automatically tense. I'm wearing my black, light cotton mix Paul Smith shirt. My gym membership runs out next week so I've been giving my pecks some extra attention, which means she can definitely feel the cut.

Definitely.

'Don't worry about your precious car,' she tells me, coquettishly. 'I'll sort it.'

As she leaves the room, I pick up her phone from the desk and wave it at her.

'Take this,' I tell her. 'If they say anything remotely sexist or demeaning to you, I want it recorded.'

In teaching we call this, using Information and Communication Technology (ICT) to Recognise and Record Progress and Achievement (RARPA). I know, it's literally a scorched earth policy of acronyms, aphorisms and euphemisms.

She bounces back into the room and takes it from me. She thinks I'm being protective; thinks I'm 'safeguarding'. I am in fact, merely after an excuse to expel the little shits for using my beautiful car as a fucking plate. This of course only serves to fuel her self-esteem. Something educationists have been drumming into the educators for decades, only to find what it actually does is fuel narcissism and depression in later life, keeping an army of NHS psychiatrists gamely employed. But you can't let empirical evidence get in the way of a lucrative public sector feed in loop.

Watching Casey's cute arse wiggle it's way between the cars gives me another idea for the college motto. I'm thinking:

'Touching Lives Forever.'

The important bullet points you should be making on Casey are these:

- She's 19 with extremely long legs
- High waist, PVC hot pants over spanx diamond sheer tights.
- Trainers over white lace frill tennis socks
- A very tight white T-shirt
- Very tight

You get the picture.

In 1974 a behaviourist called Burrhus Frederic said students will repeat desired behaviour if positive reinforcement follows. This is why I feel it is important to continually compliment the female students like Casey on their dress sense. On the T-shirt is the name of some band she told me were 'retro,' even though I could have sworn until very recently were 'rad.' They grow out so fast. I can barely keep up.

Like most of the female students around here - apart from some of the Muslim girls, Casey dresses a kind of borderline whore. On a hot day, like today, there's not so much a borderline as a mass incursion across the militarised demarcation line into unabashed sluttishness. If this were the Korean border, we'd be truly fucked.

Because of their challenged academic abilities, I insist on plenty of contact time - even with the Muslim girls. But that's the admirable thing about my libido - it's so impressively 'inclusive' it could have written the Equality Act all by itself. If I was Damian Hurst I might have even entered it for the 'Inclusive Culture Awards' before now, as a post-modern ironic statement. But I'm not Damian Hurst. For a start I can draw my own pictures and I'm not a cunt with no talent.

The kids in the car park watch Casey approach and listen intently when she speaks. One of them looks over to the window and quickly sweeps the chips onto the floor giving me an apologetic wave. This pisses me off even more - the little shit isn't even man enough to throw me the bird. I toss my cigarette out of the window and pick up the phone on my desk and speed dial the Equality and Diversity Officer. The faggot loves me; literally worships me. My courses for the last few years have been filled with enough beaver to decimate a rain forest, and more ethnic minorities than a Eurostar undercarriage. To the Equality and Diversity officer I am the dogs 'nads, and given half a chance he would lick me.

Yes, literally.

Despite appearances however, I am merely dovetailing Darwinism into my interview and selection process. That is, I naturally select only those around me who are not a threat to my alpha male status.

The conversation goes like this:

'Jeremy! Someone has defaced the Women's Month poster. I have a stu.. er, learner in front of me right now in tears; literally inconsolable!' I lie.

'Carl! Thank-you so much for bringing that to my attention! I'll have it removed immediately. Her self-esteem must be in tatters, poor thing. Have you referred her to the Pastoral Support Officer?'

I have literally no idea what a 'Pastoral Support Officer' is or does.

'Are you presuming this sort of thing can only affect female learners?!'

'Oh, God no, I didn't mean to imply that at all. Some learners undergoing gender reassignment can.. not that I'm presuming he.. or she is undergoing..'

He tails off.

'The reason I'm calling is I've just seen spray mount canisters being discarded by some learners. If you look in the bushes behind my car I think you'll find the incriminating evidence and the culprits right next to them.'

'Ah.. thank-you Carl, I'll get security on to it straight away. I hope your vigilance finally means we catch these perpetrators. It's been a constant thorn..'

I hang up.

Casey comes back into the room, closing the door behind her.

'You'd better leave that open,' I tell her. 'College policy.'

She ignores me and saunters over to my desk, looking awkward and shy - or as shy as a nineteen year old dressed as an Eastern European prostitute can look. She tells me.

'If I do that, how are you going to thank me properly for saving your lovely car?'

She moves the flowers and sits on my desk, twirling a strand of hair.

She has a point.

In education we call this, Learner Initiated Style Teaching (LIST). I look at the clock, and the professional in me is wondering whether this is a SMART move. That is - is this unscheduled extension activity as defined by the QCF Framework:

- Specific - is the activity clearly defined?
- Measurable - can the activity meet expectations?
- Achievable - is the activity easy enough for the learner to complete?
- Realistic - is the activity related to needs?
- Time Bound - Can the activity be achieved in the given time?

My next contact time isn't for another thirty minutes so yes, it ticks all the boxes nicely. Another opportunity for a 'positive learning outcome'. This is the type of deferential respect that is sorely lacking in modern higher education. And for the motto, I'm thinking:

'A Better World, One Learner At a Time.'

'Not here,' I tell her.

'Disabled toilets again?' she asks.

Oh yes indeedy.

2 BOUNDARIES

In 1985 some guy called Laird came up with this idea that learning occurred when the five senses of sight, hearing, touch, smell and taste were stimulated. If multi-senses are stimulated, he claimed, greater learning took place. What he was talking about, if you're careful enough to read between the lines, is 'sex,' and I hate to piss on his parade, but Freud came up with this shit over a hundred years earlier and called it 'deflection of the sex-impulse,' or the process of 'sublimation.' That's right, if it isn't abundantly clear by now, education is just sublimated sex, and in my humble opinion, dropping this veil of duplicity is by far the best approach to education.

Put sex right at the heart of education policy.

Learning that takes place in a charged sexual environment yields phenomenal results; why, most Nobel theories are seeded in the early twenties, when sexual drive is at its peak. It's no coincidence. In fact, John Nash's Nobel winning contributions to Game Theory resulted directly from a night on the pull; him and his nerdy mates figuring out the best way to get laid. What Laird was saying in effect was, if sex could be incorporated into every stage of the Teaching and Learning Cycle in a class full of hormone fuelled late teens, you'd have all the ingredients for an elite training establishment. It's why the oldest profession in the world can be learned so proficiently on the job. Freud even claimed this deflection of narcissistic libido was the basis for so called human civilisation. Even Germain Greer, that hypocritical clusterfuck of ever gripe ever aimed at straight white men, once proposed we should incorporate a sexual narrative into everyday life. And you can't argue with a radical feminist.

Don't even bother trying.

It's the elephant in the room of higher education theory, and frankly my own field research in this area backs it up. It scares me how far ahead of the curve I am sometimes, and if I'm not nominated for the 'Pearson's Teaching Awards' for this little nugget then it'll be yet another travesty.

Talking of which, above the new extension they've just erected a sign with the new college motto:

'Aspiring to be a Centre of Excellence - ACE.'

It's fucking awful. What degenerate sub committee could have chosen this perversion of debased, euphemistic bollocks? Even the word 'aspiring' stretches the meaning of audacity. The crowning aspiration of most colleges in the UK is, and will only ever be (at best) mediocrity. Yet the education machine habitually churns out diplomas and degrees for underachievers as if they're some alchemic fairy dust; dishing out placebo brains in the hope that they will somehow magically transform the economic fortunes of the

Land of Oz. What they should have above the door is:

'Inoffensive, Docile, Liberal Education - Thrive Without Any Talent or Skill!'

I'll leave you to work out your own acronym for that one.

My stress levels are through the roof, so I self medicate by making my regular call to the woman from 'estates' whose name I refuse to know. Like most people who work here I know them mostly as, the fat bird from accounts or the queer with the lisp. She's been sat behind the same desk for about quarter of a century with her arm elbow deep in a family size tin of 'Celebrations'. Day after day she stares at a screen, dedicating her life to making me park as far away from the college as possible, multitasking this with comfort eating her way towards a bloated public sector pension via the obesity clinic. She's reputed to have a near encyclopaedic knowledge of college policy and regulatory red tape, but ask her where the Slim-Fast is kept and she's stumped.

Obesity, as we all know, is not caused by cramming a load of sweets, cakes and carbs down your throat every day, and not getting off your fat, lazy arse to burn it all off. No, it's caused by underlying 'psychological issues'. Psychological issues are 'mental health' issues. Mental health issues, which the 'Equality Act' defines as a 'disability.' This entitles her to a whole heap of Psychiatric Help and Treatment. In other words, a PHaT tax on people like me, who stay in great shape. And correct me if I'm wrong, but I swear I didn't sign up for this crap so why do I get to pick up the bill?

I tell her that my car, (which, as I point out, is worth more than she makes in a year), has been vandalised again thanks to her. I then demand that some of the obviously over capacitated disabled parking bays be reallocated as desperately needed secure parking for people who have worked long and hard enough to afford a decent car.

It's astonishing the amount of disabled parking spaces around this place that are never occupied. Surprising on account of the amount of self diagnosed ADHD, dyslexia, dyspraxia, dyscalculia, depression, OCD, bipolar, unipolar, eating disorders, borderline personality disorders, transgender identity disorder, Asperger's, global developmental delay, underactive thyroid, overactive thyroid and whatever other normal human conditions psychotherapists and the pharmaceutical corporations decide to 'medicalise' in order to sell more drugs to incompetents.

In 1973 a psychologist called Rosenhan decided to test the accuracy of psychiatric diagnosis by sending eight perfectly sane people with false symptoms to separate psychiatric hospitals. All were diagnosed and admitted to the facilities without any problem. Immediately after being admitted they proceeded to act normally and told staff the symptoms had gone and they felt fine. Still, the average time they spend in the hospital was an amazing 19 days and were only released after being forced to admit to having a mental illness and agreeing to take a course of antipsychotic drugs.

On hearing about the experiment, an offended hospital administrator in a different hospital, challenged Rosenhan to send these 'pseudo patients' to his hospital, claiming his staff would easily be able to detect the fraudsters. Rosenhan agreed and in the following weeks staff at the hospital confidently identified 41 patients out of a 193 as being Rosenhan's fraudulent patients and a further 42 as 'suspect.' Rosenhan had in actual fact, sent no one to the hospital.

In other words, even the so called 'experts' can't decide who's making this shit up.

But I digress.

I tell the estates woman all this but she deploys her usual tactic of stonewalling me with some mythical parking allocation, or as she puts it - BS 8300, which again, correct me if I'm wrong, I didn't sign up for either. I tell her I'm sick of her BS, and demand a fucking parking space near the entrance. Granted this approach gets me nowhere, but venting my spleen like this reduces my stress levels immensely.

About half the money spent on the NHS is for preventable health issues. That's around £50 billion and rising. So if like me, everyone stayed in shape and self medicated in this way, we'd save the NHS and therefore the tax payer a fortune. It's the moral equivalent of putting solar panels on your roof to alleviate the energy crisis. If the 'Tax Payers Alliance' don't make me pin up of the year, then it'll be another Carl Waxman travesty in the making.

I hang up feeling calm, and somewhat buoyant. But it doesn't last long. Ten minutes later I hear the tick, tick, tick of Carol's body clock approaching along the corridor towards my office. Carol's official job title is 'Deputy Dean of the Faculty of Art, Design and Media,' Henry's line manger. The boss of my boss. But in truth, no-body knows what the hell she does. At 39 she's left it way, way too late. It's turned her into a complete cock snarler. Although it's not just men she hates, it's beautiful young women in the media too. Unless she thinks men are exploiting them. Then her allegiance is firmly back with the sisters.

The bullet points you should be making on Carol are these:

- She has two cats
- She drinks herbal tea and does Pilates once a week
- She believes in the healing power of crystals, reflexology and alternative medicine
- And God forbid, astrology

So desperate are women like Carol to define themselves by more than a long list of their inadequacies and dramas that they have Cats, Reflexology Alternative medicine and Pilates. In other words, a life full of CRAP. And if that isn't enough, in the absence of having a man to blame for all her fuck ups, she has astrology. Although in her world, it still doesn't let the bastards off the hook.

You get the picture.

If the psycho sirens aren't ringing already, sit up and pay closer attention. Three hundred years ago, they had trial-by-drowning to deal with women like Carol. We could learn a thing or two from that era. It's not referred to as the 'age of enlightenment' for nothing.

The local builders are in today reconstructing disabled access to a lift that can't currently be used for Health and Safety reasons, i.e. the access ramp has no handrail. I can tell the builders are in because Carol's war paint is that much thicker, her hemline that much higher, and God forbid, her ovaries are pulsing like a twin set of Peckham subwoofers. It pains me to even look at her, let alone listen to her. If I was the caring type I'd almost feel sorry for her.

But I'm not.

'Carl,' she says, folding her arms and leaning against the door-frame in a hideously misguided attempt to look 'sassy.' 'I've emailed you repeatedly about the equality and diversity course.'

She's not wrong there - six emails at last count.

'It's compulsory for all staff in the college to undertake it and forms a major part of your CPD.'

'What's CPD?' I interrupt, holding up my hand to stop her.

'CPD?! - Continuous Personal Development! You really don't know this by now?' she snorts.

God I really despise her.

'You're no exception Carl; there's an internal course starting next Monday.'

She's probably right, but I'm not going on the damn thing.

'I've registered you for it, and you will do it!'

Bitch.

'Ah,' I say, flicking through my desk diary, browsing non-existing appointments and sucking my teeth. 'Can't do I'm afraid. I've got assessments all morning, then in the afternoon I've got a meeting with Jeremy.'

Any meeting to do with equality, diversity, inclusivity, differentiation and all such bollocks are sacrosanct. They trump everything. You don't have to discuss the details. Shit meetings, compulsory courses, boring lectures; it's a get-out-of-jail-free for all occasions.

'No, you don't,' she tells me unfolding her arms. 'Jeremy's at conferences all next week; I've already checked.'

I look back at my diary doing 'perplexed', but before I can think of another excuse, she turns on her heels and leaves, triumphantly. I pick up the phone, call admissions and try to cancel my place on the course, but the sisters in admissions have already been briefed and won't let me cancel.

Bitch. Again.

I make a mental note to email her a virus. Again.

Carol's other pet hates apart from men are 'computers' and the Tech Support Department. Tech Support are usually a generation or two behind any anti-viral updates, so they'll be in her office at least a day sorting the damage out. You've got to keep people like Carol busy or they just go around making trouble for lack of having any real work to do. That's the thing about dead wood; it floats to the top. And Carol is most definitely a floater.

Looking over the shoulder of students in class will harvest at least half a dozen passwords when the work shy little shits are social networking and think I'm not looking. Carol is the type of person - the type of female who'll open any attachment where cats are involved. Adorable cats, cute kittens, dancing cats, she'll open it without a second thought, like a moth to a flame. It's not just Carol either, around the world networks are being decimated by women opening fucking cat video attachments. It's the 21st century equivalent of the black death. And you're never more than 20 feet away from a cat lover.

If the North Koreans ever want to know who's fucking with their ballistic missile program; if the Iranians ever want to know who's responsible for introducing the Stuxnet virus to their nuclear enrichment facilities, they need look no further than the innocent looking spinster sat in the corner stinking of cat piss and showing symptoms of early onset Bartonella disease. There's your culprit Ahmadinejad, right there.

Data centres currently consume 1.5 - 2% of all global electricity and are growing at 12% a year. It is becoming a major contributor to greenhouse gases. This is largely due to the uploading of cat videos. Now I'm not suggesting a complete eradication program, but wiping these pointless videos from data centres and a compulsory cull of say 99.9% of domestic cats would not only save the native bird and small mammal population in one stroke, it would also significantly reduce climate change emissions. The remaining 0.1% of cats could earn their keep in the vivisection industry, theoretical physics or eating lonely old ladies that no one wants. That's if the little bastards haven't wiped us all out with toxoplasmosis or tuberculosis first.

Yes, I'd be glad to accept a knuckle bump from the United Nations 'Champions of the Earth' award for that suggestion.

I open my email. The first two are from Carol. The cow just won't let up. The first one is to confirm my place on the equality and diversity course, the second is a general circular; a reminder that it is now department policy to use only Comic Sans on worksheets, handouts and communiqués. Apparently it makes for easier reading amongst dyslexics and other undisclosed students with 'needs'.

That's right.

This is a senior lecturer of Art, Design and Media telling us to prepare written material for the future designers and marketers of this country using the most despised font in the history of the written word. I'd rather punch a puppy in the gob than use a font associated with the public sector and Noddy.

Other things I find abhorrent:

- People who say 'literally' when they mean 'figuratively'
- People who say 'fact' after giving an obvious opinion
- People who say 'jealous' when they mean 'envious'
- People who start a sentence with 'OK' or 'So' and end it with a rising inflection
- People who say they give 110% when it's literally impossible

Comic Sans.

Fuck off.

I feel my stress levels rising again, so with my morning's work almost complete I pick up my coffee and go for a stroll to the library's computer section. I log into one of my hacked accounts and attach an infected cat video to Carol's email.

Send.

3 INDUCTION, ICEBREAKERS AND GROUND RULES

In the 1960s and 1970s a remarkable social upheaval took place. Despite being burdened with the drudgery of work and being the sole bread winner in the family, men began to realise that on returning home after a long day's slog, their women folk just weren't pulling their weight any more. So being typically pragmatic, uncomplaining and technologically advanced, men began to invent machines and services to do traditional 'women's' jobs for them. They invented washing machines, dishwashers and TV's. They invented the concept of the supermarket, home shopping, created contraceptive drugs and anti depressants. They also rolled up their sleeves and began to help out with the domestic chores, traditionally the preserve of women. They learned to cook, clean and change nappies. They even began entering labour wards to help with the disgusting mess of the birthing process, and even stayed loyal to their partners despite being made to witness the whole gruesome mess in close gynaecological detail. Is it any coincidence that nutrition and health improved as a result?

I think not.

They didn't stop there.

Men became caring fathers, expert cooks, senior nurses, head teachers and top fashion designers, picking up the slack left by women and quickly becoming experts and rising through the ranks into positions of seniority through sheer determination and hard work.

While some women raised their game and stepped up to the mark with men to move society along, others were left feeling useless, bitter, and angry which is unattractive so men, again being pragmatic, uncomplaining and technically advanced, invented the porn industry.

Threatened by the relentless resourcefulness of men, this minority of bitter, angry women formed a movement known as 'feminism.' To this day, these 'feminists' believe that women are inherently feeble and under the control of some mythical patriarchy. They believe that women can't succeed in life unless they're given special treatment, legislation and protection from the ingenuity of men. Not only do these rancorous feminists continually push for more preferential treatment, they constantly invent ever more bizarre ways to torment, demean and undermine men for being just so damned good at everything they turn their hand too.

One of the more insidious techniques is subjecting men to 'icebreakers' at the start of every emasculating training course they have ever invented.

I'm leaning back watching the arse of a seagull. It's standing on the roof light of the lecture theatre above my head. Any minute, I'm thinking, any minute now it's going to offload onto the reinforced glass, and I'm not going to blink until it does.

Fourteen minutes we've been sitting here, not that I'm counting; me and the other tutors from the various departments around the college on our mandatory 'equality and diversity' workshop day. Fourteen minutes waiting for Carol to get to grips with a Youtube video and an overhead projector.

The standoff continues; me with my Clint Eastwood eyes verses the rectal sphincter of this seagull. I can feel the dry desert heat. The theme to the 'Good, the Bad and the Ugly - Ennio Moricone's, 'Ecstasy of Gold,' starts playing in my head; both of us waiting, waiting for the other to flinch first.

Fifteen minutes. She's started to fiddle with the cables now - trying to stab a DVI-I cable into a DVI-D slot and doing untold damage to the pins. I suppose I could point out her error, but knowledge is power, no matter how trivial, so I keep it to myself. And who am I to get in the way of progress. After all, she's deputy head of the department; an advanced lecturer demonstrating how to do a job she's so eminently incapable of doing in a class no one wants to attend. I'd really hate to piss on her parade.

Then BAM! The seagull craps all over the skylight. I silently punch the air in victory and nearly fall backwards off the chair. No one sees this of course because by now, everyone is deeply engrossed in his or her own tedium detractors. No one except the middle aged woman sat next to me, who looks like she doesn't have an inner anything, except perhaps maybe a face under half an inch of war paint that she re-applies at five minute intervals.

Sixteen minutes. Sixteen minutes of my life I will never get back. The resident twelve-year-old technician has now arrived on scene to complete the humiliation by telling her she's buggered the equipment. He stomps off carrying the detritus of her ineptitude, in a vague hope of nursing it back to health.

Seventeen minutes. There's a change of plan says Carol, the red faced old munter, clapping her hands together and snapping everyone awake. We're going to skip the introductory video and go straight into the 'icebreaker.'

I fucking loathe ice breakers.

What's wrong with just setting up a tab at the local pub? It would do a far more effective job in half the time, for much less cost and effort. Lifelong friendships have been built in this way; one night stands, pregnancies even. An entire industry; an entire culture has been built around getting pissed as a universally tried and tested 'ice breaker.' Why fix what's not broken?

Pair up for ten minutes, she tells us, and interview the person sat next to you. Bullet point their name, department, length of service, and what they did before teaching; what made them want to teach and, here's the cheeky bit, find out a 'little known fact' which, she informs us, forms a humanising element that can help to break down our differences.

I don't want my differences broken down.

I like them.

They define me and separate me from the rest of the

fucking retards. I feel humiliated already. I'm partnered with Hilary and her war paint.

Here are the bullet points I make on Hilary:

- Hilary worked in a Hair and Beauty salon for twelve years
- Hilary has worked in the Hair and Beauty department for six months
- Hilary got into tutoring because she wanted to share her knowledge and experience of Hair and - Beauty with the next generation
- A little known fact about Hilary is, she once went whale watching - a prize she won through a Hair and Beauty magazine competition

Gore Vidal once said, 'The unfed mind devours itself.' Hilary is a one-woman cerebral banquette.

Here are the bullet points Hilary should be making about me:

- My name is Carl Waxman and I'm.. mid thirties.
- I have been working in the Design and Marketing department for a year where I supplicate students into participation and engagement, using obsolete ideas and non-industry standard systems and software in an impossibly liberal and politically correct environment that couldn't be further removed from the world of work if you tried.
- Before that I worked in the sales and marketing arm of JPG Investment Holdings Ltd. We didn't create anything; didn't even sell our own products or services, we just repackaged other financial products and sold them on. Even so, I was pulling

- in over £140k in pay and bonuses before the whole financial system collapsed. PPI and all the other shit you could never use? That was me.
- Why did I get into tutoring? Good question Hilary. I'm glad you asked. Because the lay offs in the financial sector were swift and the severance brutal. I had a savage mortgage on a luxury flat bought at the height of the market, which is now in negative equity, a new high end BMW with all the additional extras and certain social habits that I prefer not to discuss with you, but they don't come cheap. Why did I get in to tutoring? Because I scoured the job market for months for a proper job, but they were all gone - vanished into a recessionary ether and my creditors were breaking my balls to get another job with a regular income, no matter how pitiful. That's how I ended up here Hilary; a job of last resort, reduced to the status of a bum and even that didn't come easily in the current economic climate. I lied the hell out of my CV. You think I really want a job in the public sector Hilary? Get real.
- A little known humanising fact about myself? I regularly take my coffee breaks in the theological section of the college library, where I get an uninterrupted view of the female drama and dance students stretching and warming up before class.

I don't say this of course.

The bullet points Hilary makes about Carl Waxman are:

- Carl worked in the marketing department of a bank for several years
- Carl has worked in the college for nearly two years
- Carl decided on a change of career, because tutoring was so much more rewarding

- Carl has an interest in drama and dance

The twelve-year-old technician returns and ignoring Carol, begins setting up a new laptop and projector. Carol tells us that what we are about to see is a short but punchy vignette which supports the 'same, but different' resource pack we will be looking at later, and will help to embed a philosophy of 'equality equals quality, and quality equals equality' into our working practice while also helping the college with its 'equality-proofing' of procedures and practices.

Keep up.

And without any irony, she reminds us that education is all about simple and effective communication. She adds extra emphasis with bunny ear fingers at every God given opportunity. This isn't just painful it's politically correct water boarding. Political re-education. I swear the education sector has outsourced its entire modus operandi to North Korea.

We're handed a script on which to make notes. The lights are dimmed.

```
SCENE 01 - SCENARIO #1
FADE IN

--INT. CLASSROOM.- DAY--

BACK OF ROOM: Five students working
silently at their desks. Without
speaking, two of the students - Muslim
female - get up and leave.

CUT TO:
```

CLOSE UP: A male white student leans over to a female white student and comments.

MALE WHITE STUDENT #1
Maybe they're planning their next suicide mission. (FEMALE WHITE STUDENT GIGGLES).

MALE WHITE STUDENT #2
Don't say things like that, it's rude.

EXTREME CLOSE UP:

MALE WHITE STUDENT #1
Oh shut up, you can't talk you faggot, I saw you yesterday with your 'boyfriend.'

PULL BACK:

MALE WHITE STUDENT #2
Oh very mature, we're in the 21st Century you know. We don't get burnt at the stake any more you bigot. (TURNING TO FEMALE WHITE STUDENT). You're too good for this narrow-minded idiot.

CUT TO:

TUTOR'S POV: Both male students stand up and face off.

MALE WHITE STUDENT #1
What did you say you bender?

```
FEMALE WHITE STUDENT:
(STANDS UP) Leave it will you; what's
got into you?

CLOSE UP: MALE WHITE STUDENT #1
Nothing I'm fine

CUT TO:

BACK OF ROOM: All students sit back
down.

TUTOR
Finished?  Get back to your work!

END
```

It's all over within five minutes, but I feel scarred for life. Where was the goddamn quality control on this production? The acting, the script, the plot, everything were truly awful. The camerawork was atrocious, the lighting was abysmal, and the sound has obviously looped by non-union amateurs working without any supervision. What appeared before us bore less resemblance to a classroom environment than an amateur dramatic society's production of Snow White and the Seven fucking Dwarves.

It puts paid to the supposition that 'equality equals quality.' If I had commissioned this piece of crap I would have burned my face off in shame. From a marketing perspective, any message the film is supposed to carry is lost in the horrendous production values and I'd be amazed if a serious return on investment ever saw the light of day, unless the product placements brought in some serious up front fees.

After tea break, we're forced to endure an excruciating bout of role play, which she calls, 'situation learning' that will help us to 'make it real.' It's a bunny finger nightmare. If this is how equality and diversity are presented to the masses, and the message is in the medium, then God help community relations and multiculturalism, as rivers of blood must surely flow following this abortion.

Coercing people to act and think within an ideological framework takes flare. To mass indoctrinate or 'socialise,' takes someone with the enigmatic allure of say, Adolf Hitler or Kim Il-sung, not a middle aged munter with bad hair and bunny finger Tourette's syndrome.

In a death by power point presentation just before lunch, a second seagull lands on the skylight again. Eyes narrowing I become mercifully distracted by another feathered arsehole.

```
[You've got to ask yourself one
question:  Do I feel lucky?  Well, do
ya, punk?]
```

4 CODES OF PRACTICE

We're stood in some West End wine bar - Miles and me, trying to get served. It's one of our increasingly infrequent meet ups and he's brought a couple of skirts along from his office. I can't really afford to drink in London these days; not in these types of places, but I think of it as a business expense and a networking opportunity. Even so, I'm not trying as hard as I could to get served.

Miles is unaware of my employment situation and I need to keep it that way. As far as he's concerned, I'm working on a contract in Dubai that, a non-disclosure agreement prevents me from saying too much about. I think he buys it. If word ever gets out I've gone native; gone public sector, I'd never get a proper job again.

Apart from not being able to afford a round of drinks, the bank took back my platinum card and I don't want to be waving about the insipid piece of plastic they had the affront to send me in it's place.

'Problem is,' he continues. 'You can't even goose the office totty anymore for fear of a harassment charge, even if they do dress like a tart.'

He waves his sleek platinum over the bar at one of the waitresses. She ignores him and for a horrible moment I think she's about to serve me, but she does the pin stripe guy beside me instead.

'If you ask me, it's entrapment,' he says. 'We've got an ex-employee, putting in a harassment claim against one of the senior partners nearly four years after the event. Four fucking years! I figure it's just a way of reminding everyone she wasn't always such a dog. She actually envies her younger self. How fucked up is that?'

I shake my head in disbelief as he goes on.

'And I don't see her complaining about all the special treatment and promotions she got from blatant cock-teasing.'

He finally flags down a waitress and orders a couple of beers and a bottle of Pinot, then visibly relaxes.

'Talking of which, you still see that.. wassername. Polish bird,' he asks.

'Svetlana? Yeah, I see her from time to time, when - you know, I'm back in the UK for meetings and stuff.'

Miles nudges me in the ribs with his elbow and he looks wistfully into the middle distance.

'Yeah that's it, Svetlana. Bring her along to my party in Brighton next month yeah?'

For some weird reason his expression makes me feel possessive and a little jealous, so I take a dish of olives from the bar and start cramming them into my mouth one after the other. If I eat as much free tapas as I can, then I can at least skip the expense of dinner later.

'I thought you didn't like olives?' he says frowning at me.

It's true I don't. Cunt never misses a trick.

'Ah, you kinda get used to them in Dubai,' I tell him by way of explanation.

'So, how's life stuck out there with the dune coons?' he asks.

'Can't grumble, although there's no women in the office, they don't like getting pissed.. and drugs? Forget it.'

I roll my eyes dramatically.

'I'm actually thinking of returning to old blighty if the right opportunity presents itself,' I inform him casually.

I leave the statement hanging but the twat completely passes over the opportunity to fill the void with job offers or contacts and continues looking at the olive bowl.

'How do you get oil out of olives anyway, it's not like they're greasy is it?'

I'm starting to feel drunk myself, and we both sway a little as we stare at the bowl like it's some crystal ball, about to manifest an explanation.

'You're better off staying out of it mate,' he says finally, popping an olive in his mouth and turning back to the bar.

After punching his card number into the machine he puts a hand on my shoulder to steady himself and leans into my ear.

'Things have changed here,' he whispers loudly. 'Used to be you'd send a bird an email telling her how much you admire her tits, sometimes it got you laid, sometimes it didn't. No harm in it. If you weren't sober enough to use birth control, bosh! Babies! And that my friend is what made the world go round; how the human race went forward.'

He looks around for no apparent reason, and then leans in again.

'What we're witnessing in these modern times is an end of days, western civilization PC clusterfuck of plummeting birth rates because no-fucker is getting laid anymore for fear of litigation.'

He takes the card and receipt from the waitress, winks at her and picks up the wine and glasses and nods for me to collect the beers. We head back to the table.

'These days a simple compliment on their physical appearance can have you in front of an employment tribunal, before you can say 'rug-muncher,' he shouts back over his shoulder. 'So the resulting lack of sexual attention from men is making women increasingly frustrated and paranoid, reinforcing their bitterness and resentment towards men and exacerbating the whole fucking problem!'

He gently ricochets off people as he ploughs back to the table before plonking the bottle on the table in front of the skirt. The blonde one in the LBD looks up at me and smiles, and it starts me thinking, aye-aye.

'Let me ask you girls something,' says Miles, cutting their conversation dead.

'Have you ever met a bloke with plenty of money, a decent car, charisma, good looks and sense of humour who calls himself a feminist?'

They both giggle and shake their heads.

'Exactly. He doesn't need to. But the only way a bloke with NONE of these redeeming features is going to get laid, is to call himself a feminist and extend a companionable hand to support a lady firmly by the arse in her fight for equal rights against this apparent tyranny of men.'

He sits down heavily and takes a swig of his beer. Then in an apparent flash of epiphany adds.

'Devious cunts really; men feminists. You gotta admire them.'

*

We've been joined by more of Miles's friends; hedge fund managers and investment bankers, in a quieter bar where you can actually hear yourself talk. And it strikes me - I'm way too young to be thinking like this. These guys didn't really lose their jobs in the financial crisis, they just had them humanly recycled on the old boys' network and released back into the global economic environment. Vincent is celebrating a transfer to Shanghai.

'It wasn't greed that caused the financial crisis,' he tells me confidently, upending another empty bottle of Krug into the ice bucket beside his chair. 'It wasn't even lack of regulation. It was an ill conceived experiment in 'inclusivity."

Here's another cunt that can't stop with the bunny ears.

'It was all the rage back then - a 'customer-centric strategy' which meant bringing into the market people who were ill experienced, prepared or equipped either financially or intellectually, to handle financial responsibility and making them 'co-creators' of the financial products and services offered to them.'

He shakes his head and leans forward, like he probably does when fixing things like Libor rates

'The banking sector was pushed by a liberal elite to diversify from traditional core markets of wealthy and financially literate customers, into the cookie dough ice-cream, sweat pant trash of trailer park America. Now, it doesn't take an expert to understand that people are poor because they have NO FUCKING CLUE ABOUT FINANCE!'

A few people look up us as he takes a slug of his champagne.

'Ninja loans, sub prime mortgages? C'mon! The poor should no more be the 'co-creator' of financial products any more than they should be the 'co-creator' of my next fucking Porsche. Oi Oi!'

He knuckle bumps the guy sitting to his right and laughs.

Loudly.

The bar; it's all mosaic, mirrors and big brass lamps, like some mood lit harem. Miles is now so pissed he's lying back on the over stuffed sofa like a great Sheikh surrounded by serfs, resting a whisky on his embryonic paunch; legs splayed, eyes closed, quietly singing to the ceiling. The epitome of self satisfied contentment and entitlement like all these public school boy fuckers.

But I would.

I would do it.

I would get down on my hands and knees right now, and take a steaming great wad of his semen straight down the gullet, if it would mean me getting back a real job again. And if that doesn't prove there's equality in the work place, I don't know what does.

As so often happens on these occasions when he gets off his tits, Miles has left his platinum behind the bar on a tab, so one of the skirts has gone to order more drinks. You gotta love this guy; generous to a fault. Thanks to a strategy of minesweeping a steady stream of free nibbles from the various bars and tables, I think I'm not as pissed as I probably am. Although still, I find myself listening without complaint to Rebecca or Suzy or whatever crapping on about her gap year travels, turbo charged by repeated hops to the toilet with her girlfriends for a line or two of Charlie. It's rare to find someone who will actually listen to anyone in the City.. unless of course they're insider trading, then it's all ears.

She tells me she graduated from UCL last year and is doing an unpaid internship at the firm.

The other points to be making about Suzy or Rebecca are these:

- She works in London on no wage but still manages to support a £800 hair and beauty habit every week, with designer accessories
- She doesn't pay for any drinks or coke because she's young, beautiful so why should she?
- She thinks Miles is a 'sweetie' and he reminds her of her brother

So, he obviously hasn't shagged her yet, which is important to know as it makes her an infinitely more attractive prospect. Blowing him would be one thing, but stirring Miles's porridge would do nothing for my low self-esteem at this moment in time. By now I have hiccups and heartburn, so I'm keeping my mouth shut and appear to be nodding intermittently. She likes this, because I suspect it gives the impression that I'm listening and that we're probably connecting on some level. Somewhere between tales of Delhi and Bangkok she tails off, leans in and asks if I'll take her home. I have sunk so low in life that my immediate thought is to wonder who'll pick up the taxi fare.

Retrieving my coat from underneath Miles, he suddenly surfaces from his silent reverie.

'Did you say you're leaving Dubai?' he asks, struggling to sit up and focus on my face.

'Err, yeah. I'm thinking about it. Why?'

'Well you probably won't be interested in another offshore job, but there might be an opening in the new Shanghai office. It's not much..'

'Yeah!' I interrupt, but it coincides with a hiccup and comes out as 'Yuck!' and he waves a dismissive hand like he shouldn't have bothered me with it in the first place.

'No!' I tell him, then 'Yes! I mean yes, I'm interested. When do you want me to start?'

He pats me on the cheek, which is an achievement, seeing as he's focusing on my face about two feet behind my head.

'It's not my decision me old son,' he tells me in his mockney drawl. 'But I can put in a good word for you with Ernie Weiner on Monday. It all goes through him. Call and remind me though cos I'm pissed as a cunt and won't remember.'

And with that he lies back down.

Ching ching!

Back of the net!

I pick up a bottle of Dom Perignon, 2003 from the bar on the way out by way of celebration. On his platinum tab of course, because as Miles says, he's pissed as a cunt and won't remember. In the back of the taxi, her skirt hiked high over her hips and grinding against my leg Rebecca or Suzy tells me she has an intense urge to blow me. Right now I have an intense urge to blow myself but that's a young man's game and the back isn't what it used to be. Before she attempts to stuff my gorgeous cock into her mouth she tells me.

'We'll have to be quiet when we go in, I don't want to wake my parents.'

Parents? Suddenly I feel sixteen again. Young, fun and full of cum.

The house is one of those white Georgian terraced affairs just off Knightsbridge, with brass numbers, black railings and rising about fifty stories into the starless, sodium orange of the London night sky. By the time we've drained the last dregs of the Dom on the doorstep I just want to lie down or throw up or piss against a wall. I could quite possibly manage all three at once, but that would be just flamboyant. As soon as we're inside she starts pushing me silently and efficiently along dark corridors and up stairs telling me to be quiet, even though I swear I'm making no noise at all. I'm bundled into a bedroom where she jumps on top of me for a quiet fumbled fuck under an impossibly large duvet that smells like a chemical spill in an alpine glade, and that's it. That's me done. Granted, not exactly 'Fifty Shades,' but it has been an incredibly exhausting and emotional evening. Thank-you Rebecca or Suzy and goodnight.

*

I don't know what time it is when I wake but it's still dark and Rebecca or Suzy is asleep. I have a pounding head and badly need to piss. I wrap a bed throw around myself with trembling sweaty arms before heading for the bedroom door. Several long, long minutes of pattering up and down corridors later I still can't find any trace of a fucking bathroom, and I'm leaking like a pensioner on a day trip. What I do find is a large vase, so dropping the bed throw to the floor I pick it up and take a good long hot steaming piss into it. The relief is immensely gratifying and immediate. But this gives way to a wave of nausea, first the bile rises, then I start retching like a colic cat with a hair-ball. I bring the vase up to my face and the smell of piss punches my stomach into action. I groan and begin a spectacular bout of amplified barfing, bringing up an alcoholic soup of Bombay mix, nuts, crisps, olives and God knows what else.

When it's over I raise my head for air, I'm naked, shivering and sweating like a scouser watching Crimewatch. Then some large guy holding a metal poker at my face comes swimmingly into focus. And there's me thinking this part of London was a smokeless zone.

I drop the vase and it shatters on the parquet floor, sending ceramic shards over a surprisingly large area, and vomit and piss up both of our legs.

'I'm er.. with Rebecca,' I tell him, by way of explanation.

He steps back in disgust, shaking the piss and vomit from his Harvey Nic's slippers.

'Who the hell is Rebecca?' he snarls with a mid Atlantic accent, raising the poker higher.

'Suzy!' I tell him quickly. 'Sorry, I meant Suzy.'

He narrows his eyes further, and says slowly.

'Per-haps you mean Ra-chel?'

Shit. I'm never any good with names.

'Er yes.. Rachel. That's it. Nice hair and.. stuff.'

A women's voice, probably his wife, comes from the door behind him.

'Ernie, is everything OK darling? The police are on their

way.'

The name engages my memory. Ernie? Ernie Weiner? No way. No wonder Miles hadn't hit on the girl. She's Ernie Weiner's daughter; the boss's daughter.

Fuck.

I can see it now. Hello Mr Weiner, Miles recommended me. You may remember, we met at the weekend, I shagged your daughter under your roof without ever knowing her name, shattered some undoubtedly priceless piece of your wife's Ming Dynasty tat and covered you and your polished parquet floor in vomit and piss for good measure. But hey, how about I come work for you for a generous remuneration package?

Get real.

'I think you had better leave son,' he tells me slowly.

And with nothing left to lose - I let fly with another belly full of pick-n-mix.

5 TEACHING AND LEARNING ENVIRONMENT

I know what you're thinking:

You're thinking Carl, how does 'Maslow's hierarchy of needs' equate to success.

Are you serious?

That sort of shit is only espoused by educators with no real life experience. If you've got a proper job (i.e. not public sector) or you're successful in your chosen field, then you've probably never come across this sort of thing and wondering what the hell I'm banging on about.

Don't worry.

This nonsense doesn't effect you, because you've no doubt already worked out that real career or business success comes through hard work, adversity, pain and fear and don't need this sort of academic feminist claptrap to cloud your common sense. But it's how kids are being educated these days so maybe you'd better pay some attention, because they'll be the ones spoon feeding you porridge, wiping up your shit and beating the crap out of you at the local care home in a few years. Unless of course you're lucky enough to employ some hard working Eastern European immigrant.

It is well known that the second law of thermodynamics states that everything tends to and a dead level; to a banal, across the board conformity. What is less well known is that this is also the first law of modern education theory. It's what Hitler called 'Gleichschaltung' meaning, 'making the same', an orthodoxy designed to establish a system of totalitarian control over the masses.

Take the education theorist, Abraham Maslow for instance. When Maslow (1987) presented his hierarchy of needs in a trite pyramidal form (read from the bottom up), he argued that there were five main needs:

Maslow's Hierarchy of Needs - Education and Learning

- **Self-actualisation** - *I am achieving what I wanted!*
- **Self-esteem** - *Am I learning something useful?*
- **Recognistion** - *Do I really belong here / do others respect me?*
- **Safety / Security** - *Am I in danger while learning / am I worried?*
- **Physiological** - *Is my learning environment comfortable / am I hungry, thirsty, tired or cold?*

It's rumoured this was originally lifted from a Spartan training manual.

Not.

Interestingly, in this 'educational' version that I ripped out of a tutor training text book from the library before binning it in disgust, 'needs' has been cleaned up by the feminist author who has omitted 'sex', which as I have already pointed out forms a fundamental part of the teaching and learning cycle.

This 'Maslow's hierarchy of needs' might work fine for four year olds, but it also forms the framework which underpins all modern education and training up to adulthood. If these needs are not met, Maslow claimed, then the individual will feel anxious, tense and will not be motivated into learning, success or achievement.

I know.

Bullshit righ?

Sumner Redstone, the media magnate once said.

'Success is not built on success. It's built on failure. It's built on frustration. Sometimes it's built on catastrophe.'

Jordan Belford put it more personally.

'When you do something, you might fail. But that's not because you're a failure. It's because you have not learnt enough. Do it differently each time. One day, you will do it right. Failure is your friend.'

'Failure is your friend.'

Goddamn right Mr Belford you God amongst men, sir.

But let's leave Abraham Maslow's pyramid in the toilet

where it belongs and turn to some real manly stuff like Francis Ford Coppola movies.

Now we're talking.

What can the making of the film, 'Apocalypse Now' teach us about success, achievement and life? If you answered 'everything', you'd be spot on. If not you probably work in - I don't know, the HR department of a local council and worse still, proud of the fact.

Seriously, sort your shit out, dickweed.

Apocalypse Now is quite simply the greatest movie ever made and forms a framework exemplar to goal attainment in the face of adversity.

How so Carl?

I'll tell you.

Based loosely on Joseph Conrad's novella, 'Heart of Darkness,' Apocalypse Now was set during the Vietnam war and grossed over $150 million world wide. Considered a modern masterpiece by critics who obviously know about this sort of thing, it is frequently cited as one of the greatest movies ever made and has won numerous awards, including three Golden Globe Awards, two academy Awards and the Cannes Film Festival's Palme D'Or to name but a few. In short it was a 'success.' Or as Abraham Maslow might have put it, Francis Ford Coppola 'self-actualised.'

Fuck sake.

It also had helicopter gun ships and Playmates, so seriously, what's not to like? But it didn't start out that way. At the outset, Marlon Brando didn't want anything to do with Coppola after the Godfather movies. So Coppola offered him a million dollars a week, plus a cool million upfront to persuade him to get his fat arse into shape and play the part of Walter E. Kurtz, the renegade colonel.

In the script, Colonel Walter E. Kurtz was an enigmatic, war hardened, lean fighting machine; a special forces colonel who had gone insane, but when Brando turned up on set, he was a twenty stone, disorientated monstrosity, who was drunk and had done absolutely no research on his character or made any attempt to get in shape for the part. So the cast and crew stood down for several weeks while Coppola personally wheedled and cajoled some form of credible performance out of the idiosyncratic legend. Even so, he had to be filmed in deep shadow in a smoked filled temple, with only his head and shoulders in shot to disguise his elephantine proportions, the fat fuck.

Brando was like the spoilt, special needs, obese kid of the production that swallowed up a massively, disproportionate amount of resources and money for very little gain.

Furthermore Brando refused to appear on set with Dennis Hopper who was playing an eccentric Photojournalist. This didn't bother Dennis Hopper however; because he was so spaced out he could barely speak coherently, let alone remember any lines.

Harvey Keitel, playing Willard, the main character was sacked after only two weeks of filming to be replaced by the little known Martin Sheen who had an alcohol induced mental breakdown on set. He admitted later:

'That opening sequence was shot on my 36th birthday, and I was so drunk I couldn't stand up.'

What a man.

He subsequently went on to suffer a heart attack and was doubtful about living to see the end of filming.

Helicopters, hired in from the Philippine government were whisked away mid filming to fight communist insurgents leaving the cast and crew standing around bemused and wondering what the hell was going on and whether they'd ever return. A typhoon ripped through the sets reducing them to ruined quagmires of mud and destruction that set the schedule back several months, and pushed the production way over budget.

By this time, Coppola had strayed so much from the original script that, by the end of filming, many of the day's shooting schedules simply read, 'scenes unknown,' and the actors had to resort to improvisation. Some of the cast and crew were so stoned and drunk they simply didn't care while others were in abject despair.

When the original scriptwriter, John Milius showed up on set, they begged him to talk some sense into Coppola. However, Coppola had sunk into a deep depression of his own by this time. With his career, reputation and entire wealth riding on the film, he was by now going through a deep personal crisis. Facing artistic and financial bankruptcy, he admitted the film was a disaster and that he was thinking of shooting himself. Originally budgeted at $12 million with a six-week shoot, the movie had ballooned to a cost of $30 million and finally ended up taking sixteen months.

When filming was finally complete, there were well over a million feet of negatives - 230 hours of footage.

Approximately ten per cent of that was Kilgore's helicopter gunship attack alone. Coppola figured on there being about a 20% chance of success in editing it into some form of coherent structure. Out of Brando's eighteen-minute inarticulate ramblings Coppola managed to salvage two minutes of usable footage and Sheen was brought back to dub a voice over, in a desperate attempt to knit the narrative together. It took nearly three years to edit it into the film we know and love today.

When it was all over, Francis Ford Coppola confessed:

'My film is not a movie. My film is not about Vietnam. It is Vietnam. It's what it was really like. It was crazy.'

But adversity is how greatness is achieved and legends are created. Clearly when Coppola was sitting in a jungle with his film constantly teetering on the edge of disaster and he, himself bordering on madness, was he scrutinising Abraham Maslow's little pyramid for inspiration? Was he ringing up his pastoral support officer, claiming discrimination or bitching about his physiological environment and security impeding his progress?

Was he fuck.

With a typhoon raging around him, and staring into a reputational and financial abyss he manned up, grew a pair and became motivated as hell by a grim determination not to fail.

In her diary at the time, Coppola's wife observed, 'It's scary to watch someone you love go into the centre of himself and confront his fears, fear of failure, fear of death, the fear of going insane. You have to fail a little die a little, go insane a little to come out the other side.'

Goddamn right Eleanor, now go write some educational theory textbooks!

So what can the making of Apocalypse Now teach us about education and life? For a start it proves educationalists know bugger all about the psychology of achievement and success. Goals are not realised by referring to some euphemistic pyramid of platitudinal shite. Shame and embarrassment are cited as the very building blocks of societal living. Hardship and the fear of real failure are the key motivational force and a prime catalyst in man's greatest achievements. If you can't fail, how can you ever hope to win?

Coppola himself admitted, 'There is a kind of powerful exhilaration in the face of losing everything.'

Through the pen of John Milius, Martin Sheen's character, Willard, put it even better.

```
[Charlie didn't get much [leisure
time]. He was dug in too deep or
moving too fast. His idea of great R&R
was cold rice and a little rat meat.
He had only two ways home: death, or
victory.]
```

Holy mother of God, someone check my pants because I think I've just cum.

6 LEARNING STYLES

'Come on, it's nearly one,' I tell Henry.

Torn between hunger and an ill-conceived diet, Henry pushes a limp salad around his plate with a plastic fork in a last minute, futile attempt to find fortification and sustenance.

'Stick it in a bun and bring it with you,' I tell him impatiently, the weekend's excess still gnawing at the back of my brain.

He shakes his head. With the sad, defeated dejection of a surgeon who has lost a patient, he staggers to his feet. With that air of special foreboding only a departmental meeting can confer, we leave the cafeteria pausing only briefly for Henry to grab a Mars bar and diet coke from the vending machine.

I notice Karen, the Fashion course leader, coming through the entrance lobby carrying a baby sling. Karen has been on maternity leave for over two years with a brief interlude in between in which she got herself knocked up again, but nevertheless is still invited to sleep and breast feed through departmental meetings and punctuate them with nappy changing and crying to 'keep her in the loop.'

I fall into step behind her and note the incredible amount of weight she has gained as she ambles down the corridor. This almost makes me feel sad for her but to a greater degree, for her husband who obviously didn't foresee this sort of thing happening (always in these situations, look to the mother-in-law for the warning signs). Then I quickly decide it's his own damn fault for breeding in the first place. This no longer makes me feel sorry for him, and that makes me feel better. I'm never fully comfortable with sympathy anyway, so that's fine.

Henry brings up the rear, dragging his feet like the asthmatic fat kid on sports day, puffing at his ventilator. Henry has of late become the department's piñata. Like bestiality porn, it doesn't really give you any great pleasure to watch, but it is kinda mesmerising anyway.

Like Spring Watch I guess.

Doris Lessing once said, 'Men are the new silent victims in the sex war, continually demeaned and insulted by women without a whimper of protest.'

I'm positive Doris had Henry in mind when she said this, but had she attended just one of these departmental meetings, she would have endorsed my strategy of non-engagement wholeheartedly.

As always 'Apocalypse Now' puts it more succinctly:

```
[- Why do all you guys sit on your
helmets?
- So we don't get our balls blown
off.]
```

I kid myself it is the kind of passive resistance that Mandela, Ghandi or Jesus would endorse, but in reality, I'm probably just a coward and in all honesty, they were probably all just pussies too.

History is very forgiving.

Henry has never understood that meetings are not about decision-making or the democratic process. All decisions are made before-hand by secretive conspiratorial subgroups. Meetings are there to reinforce hierarchy and to add fuel to the fire of any forum flame wars and to ignite new threads. When the meeting is predominated by feminists, it is doubly so and the meeting takes on a particular sense of perniciousness, dysphoria, length and futility. Brevity and clarity? Forget it.

The best strategy to adopt in such circumstances is to expect nothing, say nothing, and do nothing. Sit on your helmet so your balls don't get blown off. Think hibernation, and you're half way there. The only time your name should ever appear on the minutes of a departmental meeting is either under the heading 'present' or 'apologies.'

Preferably 'apologies.'

The dedicated meeting rooms were converted into IT rooms years ago, so meetings are now held in the long thin 'room' known as the 'mezzanine' - an extra floor built above the screen printing studio to create extra 'affordable' space for the college. If you're anything taller than a midget, you have to walk in the centre of the room to avoid the rafters.

On the south side are long glass dormer windows, which means the place heats up like a tropical palm house in summer and freezes like a brass-monkey ball remover in winter. The opposite wall/roof is hung with student work, which constantly peels off due the extreme temperature fluctuations. Coupled with the fact that railings offer no sound insulation from the screen-printing workshop below, you have all the ingredients for the shittest possible environment in which to hold a meeting. And when a meeting room smells of herbal tea and rice crackers, you know any rationale is already lost.

Student reps from each year of every course already occupy the more comfortable seats, then the small procession of Fashion tutors arrive fashionably late, after making all the decisions in a pre-meeting meeting. Dr Jones, the 'Chair' who is a man and therefore always punctual, has rearranged his row of pens and shuffled his annotated agenda several times already. By the time, everyone has cooed over Karen's baby, commented on each other's weight loss 'Really?' new clothes, 'What these old things?' sweat beads are appearing on brow of Dr Jones as he begins scratching the back of his neck with the fixed smile of a Cheshire cat being slowly neutered with a butter knife.

To his left is Jeremy, the Equality and Diversity officer who is present at all departmental meetings in line with college procedure, the records of all past meetings, separated with colour co-ordinated paper clips in front of him. To the right of Dr Jones sits the distractingly obese woman from 'estates' who does the minutes with a barely concealed packet of Maltesers which she discretely pops into her mouth during the lulls. Finally we're all huddled together around the makeshift conference table.

So many freaks, but alas, so few circuses.

The clock on the wall tells me it's already 1:23pm.

Carol opens the meeting by asking if anyone minds if she opens a window. She obviously doesn't need to ask as it's stiflingly hot, but she always addresses meetings first as a kind of territorial pissing exercise before anyone is under the misconception that the 'Chair' who is a man, is in charge. However, she is somewhat undermined by the fact that Henry jumps up to help her when he sees her struggling, as she always does with anything 'technical.' He sees this as being gentlemanly and hopes it will help somewhat ease Carol's animosity towards him. She sees this as him being an interfering patriarchal cunt.

The printers clatter below punctuated by the loud swearing of students as they simultaneously wrestle with the ancient equipment and facilitate everyone with the painfully banal social arrangements of themselves and their favourite celebrities. They find it hard to distinguish.

'Kim Kardashian!? she was like, OMG you are sooo gay!'

'Gay.' It's one of those words that I can never remember if it's homophobic, has been reclaimed or is acceptable in a post ironic context. I'll have to check my memos on that one. The other tutors look equally as conflicted and confused on how to address this blatant use of a 'word', so they all look to Dr Jones for leadership on the matter.

Dr Jones, his neck scratched raw from frustration sighs,

stands up and like a Greek God who really cannot be fucked with the affairs of humanity anymore, shouts down something banal and non committal to make them shut up.

Finally he brings the meeting officially to order, signing off the minutes of the previous one. If I hadn't waited for Henry, I could have bagged one of the more comfortable seats under the windows that the fucking students now occupy and be asleep by now.

But I didn't.

So I'm not.

I never read the minutes, firstly because I'm not the least bit interested and will never contribute and secondly.. No that about sums it up really. The Fashion, Hair and Beauty contingent however fizz and buzz with excitement, in anticipation of their pre-dawn raid on the agenda being rubber-stamped by the meeting.

The number one item on the agenda is the seeming inability to attract a sizeable number of 'ethnic minority' students to the department's courses.

'This is a major embarrassment to us all,' Carol tells us. 'A representative mix of British multi-cultural ethnicities is essential to show we're a modern forward thinking department.'

After telling us how we're all feeling about the matter, she proposes a kind of positive discrimination, in which quota's are set for minority groups. Jeremy tells her that it's not 'positive discrimination' anymore as that's now illegal, it's 'positive action' which is basically the same thing but - you know, using different words. Henry however in a misguided sense of reassurance, points out that the local area is void of any sizable 'ethnic minority' group. The college's catchment area, he tells them is predominantly white and the few Asia students that do attend the college tend to favour more business orientated courses anyway. Jeremy tells him the term 'white' holds connotations of power and imperialism amongst some minority groups but is unsure of the correct term to use, as there are no positive denotations for 'whites' unless perhaps it has the suffix, 'female' so he's sorry to interrupt.

'Please carry on.'

Carol accuses Henry of racial stereotyping, but Jeremy chimes in, reminding the meeting of the fact that Design and Marketing - our course - has enrolled more 'ethnic minorities' than any other course within the department. Carol throws Jeremy a withering look, pointing out that Design and Marketing isn't, in her opinion, an 'Art' subject anyway - it should be hived off to Business and Administration department. Jeremy points out that this kind of backs up Henrys first point. The meeting collapses into a mess of exponentially bifurcating conversations until Mary, the only visible 'minority' in the room and Hair and Beauty course leader, brings a heavy Ghanaian hand down on the table, that shakes the entire mezzanine floor like the hammer of Thor. There's certainly nothing 'minority' about her.

Mary was once a model - and again I start feeling sad for her husband here because he married her before the rot set in, but then remember my change of policy on the matter. Being one of the few black members of staff at the college she divides her time between lecturing and trying to avoid publicity shots for the college prospectus, to prove its multi-ethnic credentials. However, as far as she's concerned, the photo-shoots merely document her rise in weight and shattered modelling career. The fact we are all contracted to do any publicity shots for free at the behest of management, merely rubs salt in a gaping wound.

Just as being a victim of crime doesn't make you an expert criminologist, being of a different skin colour doesn't make you an expert sociologist or geneticist, but still, your argument will always carry more weight when talking on the subject, particularly if you're surrounded by white sycophantic liberals. It is, in it's own peculiar way the worst form of patronising, racial stereotyping there is if you think about it.

Mary suspecting the approach of another photo-shoot, flips her hand in the air and 'pftss.'

'Why you always tark about dis?' she asks looking at everyone accusingly. 'You people always tark, tark tarking about skin colour. I want no tark about dis ridiculous ting. God does not see colour, he see only people.'

Again she 'pftss' heavily and flips a dismissive hand in the air, and as if by some queer voodoo magic and invoking God, she makes the point completely disappear.

Next up is Jeremy's item about posters being defaced. He thanks me in particular for bringing the matter to his attention, 'Thank you for your continued vigilance Carl,' and says that women's month has been blighted by the pernicious graffiti of a minority of students who oppose such campaigns. Which is ironic seeing as the last point was all about encouraging minority students; minorities are obviously to be discouraged now.

It's a very confusing state of affairs.

He goes on to say that he fully understands the financial pressures on everyone, but he has secured contributions from other departments to buy locked display cabinets made from thickened, none reflective glass and sustainably sourced wood for future poster campaigns, to stamp out dissent in the name of tolerance.

I've always found the use of the word 'tolerance' a bit of an oxymoron in terms of racial prejudice. Surely a term that refers to endurance or forbearance, such as 'tolerance of pain / noise / cold' etc., suggest a deviance from something more preferable, or am I just missing something? Maybe liberals are covert racists after all.

No objection is aired and a lengthy discussion ensues on the subject of Primark and cakes for some reason, that I completely fail to follow. By now I've lost the will to live.

It is decided that the department could forgo the planned purchase of essential projection equipment, in the interest of a much worthier cause - display cases. After all, as any North Korean official will attest, education is first and foremost about social engineering and indoctrination, not pedagogic endeavour and budget allocation should always reflect this. Jeremy is delighted by the result and informs us they can be ordered and installed in time for 'domestic abuse' month. It could have all ended there and moved on, but no, Henry raises his hand.

'Why focus on just one type of violence?' he suggests helpfully. 'Why not have an all encompassing anti-violence month?'

Oh Henry, Henry, Henry. Why can't you just shut the fuck up and look out of the window like the rest of us.

There's an intake of breath from several quarters.

[Never get out of the boat, unless you're goin' all the way]

'Are you saying violence against women isn't an important issue for you Henry?' asks Carol.

'No, not at all, it's very important, but I was reading in the Guardian just this morning that violence is overwhelmingly directed towards young men. My nephew was attacked only last month on a night out with friends and it got me thinking...'

Jeremy, seeing Henry's balls firmly locked in the crosshairs of the feminists, intervenes.

'Domestic violence is an issue that affects both men AND women so..'

'But overwhelmingly women,' interrupts Carol.

'Most reported domestic abuse yes, but...'

'And what about the hidden statistics? Whose side are you on anyway Jeremy?' asks Jenny, the acting Fashion course leader, with her head cocked to one side, taking aim.

'I'm on no-one's side, I'm just pointing out that domestic violence isn't necessarily a gender based issue.'

And suddenly Jeremy's balls appear in the cross hairs too. He's only got himself to blame. I could show some solidarity here, but I don't want my balls decorating the interior of the mezzanine, so I continue to sit on my helmet.

'Can we stick to the agenda here gentlemen!... and ladies... ladies and gentlem.. people!' says the 'Chair' who is a man. 'It's been over an hour already and we've barely made a dent in the agenda.'

Outside the sun slowly moves across the sky, and inside the temperature rises. Seats shuffle to avoid the glare from the windows. I'm faintly aware of a smell, which at first my subconscious puts down to the presence of so many hot hairy feminists in a confined space, that no amount of herbal tea and rice cakes can mask, but even they couldn't possibly produce a smell like this.

Could they?

I look around for the source and it seems to be coming from the sleeping, prone mass of Karen. Oh God, I think, she's actually shat herself with sheer boredom. But then the increasingly restless baby in the pop up carry-cot beside her reveals ground zero. In the heat, the smell increases to indescribable levels. Seats begin to inch away and discrete hands go up to faces. Yet in this day and age of ubiquitous offence, where even the most innocent remark is grist to the mill of the affrontorati, no one even acknowledges it. (The affrontorati is a bit like the illuminati.. but way more insidiously powerful).

Henry's forgotten mars bar begins to wilt in his pocket and the students are lost too deep, deep within their mobile phones to notice anything. If someone doesn't do something soon, I'm seriously going to puke, and I ponder on the etiquette of elbowing a sleep-deprived mother in the fucking ribs to wake her up. It's no wonder that two out of three of the gifts the Magi brought when visiting the baby

Jesus were potent aromatic resins. Christian's call them 'gifts', but let's be honest; it's a bit like bringing a 'gift' of ear-plugs along to a child's piano recital. They weren't known as 'wise men' for nothing. Although the guy with the gold must have felt like a right twat.

The temperature rises even further, heads begin to loll and the baby's whingeing increases. Still, nothing. Karen sleeps, and the meeting drags inexorably on.

And on.

Suddenly, Mary stands up with the irascibility of a woman made to sit through Jeremy Clarkson explaining the offside rule during a long haul flight.. on Ryanair. There's a flurry of student phones being stuffed into bags and lolling heads snap to attention as she stomps around the table, 'pfft'-ing all the way. She sweeps the baby up in one hefty arm and the nappy bag in the other and muttering under her breath marches from the room with both.

Still Karen sleeps on.

There's stunned, embarrassed silence.

'I'll open another window,' says Carol, seizing the initiative to vicariously claim a victory for women through Mary's actions - as she does with any female achievement, no matter how trivial.

'Mary has a mother's instinct,' she says, struggling with the window catch. 'And a woman's intuition.'

There are nods of agreement, and buoyed by the other sisters who are rallying to her cause, she adds;

'If only men would take the initiative sometimes and be a little more pro-active.'

Henry seeing this as a veiled invitation to help her with the window, stands up to help.. then immediately sits down again when he sees the expression on her face.

And I'm thinking, a man would never drag a sleep deprived mother with a weaning infant through an 'ordeal by futile meeting' in the first place. He would use his man brain to send her the minutes using manmade technology to her manmade house, via the manmade Internet or stream the whole fucking thing via a manmade webcam or conference call. He would never hold a coffee morning under the thinly veiled guise of a meeting in the first place. That would be a father's instinct Carol. That would be a man's intuition Carol.

Fuck sake.

Besides, any man would be in fear of his life if he picked up the baby of a sleeping mother and walked out of the room with it. It's why so few men volunteer to run scout groups or kids activities anymore. It just takes one women to point a finger and shout 'Where's your CRB check!' and for the rest of your life, you're at best, a social pariah or at worst picking up soap in the prison shower for your new wife, Mr Big.

Mary re-enters the room and deposits the now sleeping baby into Henry's arms, I guess in the belief that having two kids makes him eminently more capable than anyone else. However, what she probably doesn't know is Henry was thrown out of the house by his wife when the kids were only just out of nursery, as he wasn't seeing to her 'emotional' needs. It seems the builder, contracted to do the extension on their house was seeing to her 'emotional' needs while Henry was at work seeing to her 'financial' needs. An arrangement that continues to this day, keeping her in a £400k house with her kids, two incomes and no job and him renting a bedsit paying maintenance and having fortnightly access during which the kids continually harass him for sweets, money and fucking computer games.

Hands on hips, Mary glares accusingly at the other women and cuts to the chase.

'What is wrong witchoo?! You never change a nappy before? Pfsst. What good your degrees and all your tark if you can no even change a baby nappy for another woman?'

Mary belongs to a branch of feminism known as 'womanism' which is in itself a derivative of 'post colonial feminism' and a branch of 'women of colour'

Keep up.

Like most feminists, she wouldn't be averse to seeing men publicly castrated for no other reason than her own amusement, but it's nothing to the animosity she feels towards white metropolitan feminists, with their 'Eurocentric ideals' and 'separatist agenda' as she puts it. This leads to confusion within the feminist camp as no-one can agree on anything other than hating men under the guise of 'inequality' even though 'inequality' has been illegal for a long time and can be addressed through the law courts anyway. Unless of course it's men who are being discriminated against in the family courts.

Then it's fine.

You can follow the fascinating cut and thrust of modern,

feminist thinking on twitter under the hashtag - whoinGodsnamereallygivesafuck. Alternatively if you want to see a bunch of lesbians slugging it out in a more engaging manner, the Internet is full of such videos.

Mary knocks Carol from the window with her immense hips and with one almightily pull on the window bar, brings the entire window away from its frame. It crashes to the floor and the shattered remains bounce through the railings and over the side of the mezzanine. The cacophony and screams from below wake up Karen (finally), who after a brief interlude of disorientation, looks to the carry-cot to see her baby vanished.

Seeing everyone's attention focused over the railing she immediately presumes her baby has made a dive for freedom to the floor below and races for the stairs, giving vent to a primal scream that would put Boadicea to shame.

On seeing Karen's distress, Henry jumps up from his chair and holding the baby at arms length follows her to the stairs calling after her. Karen whips around and on seeing Henry with her baby, snatches it from him and for no reason I can figure, slaps him so hard across the side of his head it actually perforates his eardrum, ratifying his earlier point that most violence is indeed directed towards men.

It takes a good half hour to soothe the distressed Karen and get her into a taxi, with Carol re-assuring her it was all a misunderstanding; probably Henry's fault anyway.

That's right.

When it comes down to it Henry, you were probably asking for it anyway - you bitch.

7 KEY THEORIES OF LEARNING

The celebrity, Whitney Houston once said that she believed children were the future, before banqueting on cocktail of cocaine, marijuana, Benadryl, Xanax, and Flexeril and diving into a very deep hot bath. Like Amy Winehouse, her death was not labelled 'fucking dumb', but a 'tragic accident.' It's no wonder kids are confused by the mixed messages on drugs. However, looking at the manner of her death, perhaps 'Greatest Love of all' wasn't intended as a melodious homage to our future generation or about self-love. It was probably just a very tuneful, chart topping suicide note.

If you look around at our education system and still truly believe that children are our future, as Whitney did, you'd probably take a bucket full of barbiturates and run yourself a very deep hot bath too.

I'm stood outside, hiding from the rain in the smoking shelter with some students, staring through the graffiti at the car park. I blow a slow stream of contemplative grey smoke into the grey mist. In moods like this, when final reminders, and the world in general are against me, I find it sometimes helps to stare at my car, parked in one of the disabled bays, and remind myself that serenity and beauty can still exist in the world. But through the damp air I make out a note attached to the windscreen.

The woman from estates has been at my car!

Stomping over, I snatch the offending object from behind the wipers only to find it's not a ticket at all, but a hand written note neatly sealed inside a plastic sandwich bag.

'We really need to meet,' it tells me. 'Cafe Rouge in the High Street at 4:30pm.'

That's it, no 'please'? My first thought is that finally, the flower sender is going to reveal herself, but why not send a note with the flowers or just put it in my mail tray in the corridor? Better still why not just send an email like normal people have done for millennia?

The rest of the day pans out in its banal inevitability, although I can't get the note out of my mind. Why the mystery? The words, 'we really need to meet,' can only mean bad news. Pregnancy? Emotional blackmail? Threat? Another student with a declaration of love? Surely these would be accompanied by 'You'll learn something to your advantage.' 'You'll regret it if you don't,' or 'I'll kill myself if I can't be with you!'

I set the collar of my Burberry Brit Eckford Pea Coat against the wind and leave. It's looking a bit scuffed these days; a bit battered and bruised, but it's still the most stylish item on campus, and that includes anything the Fashion department can come up with. Even by Ebay prices it would finance the restoration of a small African village.

I know.

I read a poster.

If ever I was lost in Africa with no money, I could sell the coat and be fine. This thought comforts me.

Buoyed by this modicum of opulent superiority, I take the back exit of the college grounds and make the ten-minute walk to the high street leaving the car in the college car park to avoid the parking charges in town. Cafe Rouge is probably at the high end of the cafe franchise in the street, which tells me it's probably not a student that left the note.

That would be Nando's at best.

On entering I unbutton the top button of my coat and casually scan the interior for a familiar face, not sure whether to set my own face to 'irritated,' 'apologetic,' or 'contrite,' to suit the situation. It's not good to begin meetings on the back foot; you need to get into role. A few people look up then back down to their coffees, but then some rich looking GILF in a camel skin Armani trench jacket, who I swear I've never met in my life, let alone slept with, gestures to the vacant seat at her table. At least pregnancy is off the cards.

'Mr Waxman,' she says, standing up and shaking my hand when I get to the table. 'I'm so pleased you decided to come, I've already ordered. Would you like to..?' she asks, gesturing to the waiter, who has already appeared by the table.

'Cappuccino,' I tell him.

Then it occurs to me. She could be the mother of one of my students - Casey maybe, and again all possibilities are back on the table.

'In the interest of brevity and courtesy Mr Waxman, I'd like to lay my cards on the table straight away. I do not hold a grudge, neither am I vindictive. Do you have a wife or girlfriend at present?'

'What? No, why?'

'Good, one would hate to see any more lives destroyed. What about children?'

'Er, not as far as I know,' I tell her with a nervous grin, that shows her I have a lighter side, but fails miserably to crack a smile.

'Sorry. Bad joke. What's this about Mrs.. ?'

'Of course; how rude of me. I haven't even introduced myself. My name is Bethany. I am Rachel's mother.'

Shit, it is about a student. The name 'Rachel' rings a bell but the rest of my memory banks are silent.

'Rachel Weiner?' she offers. 'Or perhaps you remember her better as Rebecca or Suzy?' she continues, teasing out a latent memory like it's some mentalist hiding behind a sofa.

Oh shit. Oh shit, oh shit, oh shit. She's pregnant. Oh shit again. Ohhhh shhhiittt!

'How.. er, is Rachel?' I ask, my heart suddenly pounding like a bunny on Viagra.

'Oh, so so,' she says wavering a hand.

'It takes time to recover from these things.'

'Recover from what?' I ask, thinking perhaps she's already had the abortion - thank God.

That's it, she's had an abortion and her mother is here to vent her spleen; call me a callous shit or something. Anything. I don't care; I'll take it on the chin, whatever it is, as long as she's not pregnant. The last thing I need right now is a bill for child support.

'Rape,' she says casually.

'Shit!' I say, genuinely taken aback.

'I'm, sorry. God that's awful. When?'

'Oh come now Mr Waxman, my daughter may have been inebriated but you were in full control of your faculties on the night that you took advantage of her.. hospitality. Liberally covering both her and my home with, how shall I put it – DNA evidence?'

The waiter arrives with the cappuccino. I just stare at her open mouthed. This has got to be some joke.

'But she invited me back and took me straight to bed. She even went on top because I was way too exhausted to - you know, perform.'

Even under the circumstances it seems a bit crude to spell out the voracity of a daughter's libido to her own mother.

'The law does not require the victim to have physically

resisted in order to prove a lack of consent Mr Waxman. Our family lawyer is quite clear on the subject. His firm represents the Duchess of Cambridge you know? He's very exclusive and expensive, but oh so knowledgeable and competent in these matters. Some would say ruthless, but he's just a great big teddy bear really when you get to know him.'

'I would have just been happy to sleep. It had been a very emotional evening!' I protest.

'A woman consents if she agrees by choice, and has the freedom and capacity to make that choice. The phrase you fail to understand Mr Waxman, is 'agreement by capacity.' May I call you Carl, it's so much less formal? My daughter had been given a substantial amount of drink and drugs that evening – none of which she bought herself. She didn't have the capacity to give her consent, ergo, no consent was given.'

She leans across and slowly tells me.

'By the lawful definition of the word Mr Waxman, it was most definitely rape.'

I undo another button on my jacket and take a sip of the cappuccino, spilling some on my hand. I don't even feel it. I need to rally here or I'm fucked. The best form of defence is attack. I read that someplace.

'If anyone was raped it was me!' I tell her. 'I didn't even.. I mean, she went on top!'

She reaches across and with a silk handkerchief, wipes the cappuccino froth from my shaking hand and smiles.

'Carl,' she says with the assurance and confidence of someone who has known money, privilege and superiority all of her goddamn life. 'An act of rape can only be performed by a person with a man-penis. It's lawfully impossible for a woman to rape a man.'

'Well that's.. ' I struggle for the right word. 'Sexist,' I say eventually, realising how pathetic it sounds but still trying to maintain some dignity.

She raises her hands in submission.

'Don't shoot the messenger dear, I don't make the laws.'

'But she blew me in the taxi on the way home then pushed me into bed when we got there. That must imply some sort of consent?'

She quickly withdraws her hand and looks at me with horror.

'Are you saying a charge of sexual assault from earlier in the evening should be considered too? I really must expand my legal team.'

I try to go to my calm place, and desperately try to create some Buddha time. What would Willard's advice be?

[Oh man... the bullshit piled up so
fast in Vietnam, you needed wings to
stay above it.]

Which is no fucking use whatsoever.

She takes a sip of her black Americano, no sugar. Watching me. Waiting. Waiting for what? Finally she sighs.

'As I said at the beginning Carl, I am not vindictive. I'd hate to see two young lives ruined over an evening of, how shall we describe it, 'sexual misadventure?' Rachel is a sensitive soul, easily swayed into relationships with unsuitable men.'

She twists the handkerchief into a tight ball in her hand.

'Especially those bastards from Ernie's work who see a trusting face and pretty smile and.. trade her, like she's just another commodity.'

She takes a deep breath.

Calm.

'But, I've been watching you Carl; studying you. I can see you're a principled fellow at heart. You've left the financial sector behind and taken up a good solid career in teaching. I find it admirable when people turn their back on the pursuit of wealth and just follow their calling; their vocation in life. It shows maturity.'

She double taps my hand.

'By the way, you may want to change your LinkedIn profile, it says you're still working in Dubai.'

'Oh, er, yeah. Oops, I really need to update that don't I? Thanks.'

Taking a sachet of sugar, she opens it and deposits half into her cup, before stirring it slowly.

'I can see in you, the type of man who could make my

Rachel happy. Now if you two were to say.. make a go of it, then perhaps I may be persuaded that I have.. misinterpreted your actions on that night; that your graceless entry into my daughters life and my home were in fact born from a deeper desire to make her happy on a more.. long term basis.'

Her delivery is calm and slow, but my mind is racing to keep up with the intimations of her words. I pick up my cup and put it down again. Then pick it up again, leaving it to hover half way to my lips.

'You want me to.. date Rachel?' I ask, puzzled; disgusted even, but relieved we've moved on from the rape allegation.

'Would that be so bad Carl? Rachel is a lovely girl wouldn't you agree?'

How could I not?

'Well, yes obviously. Absolutely. Lovely.'

This is nuts.

'Could I talk to Rachel about this maybe?' I ask innocently.

'Rachel needs some space at the moment to help her gain a clearer understanding of her situation, just as the sexual offence liaison officer advised her to do. She is in a very confused emotional place at the moment. What she needs now is love, support and the promise of a more stable future.'

I can feel the hopelessness of the situation beginning to overwhelm me. I could get a lawyer. I can't afford one but maybe I could get legal aid? Haven't they cut the legal aid budget though?

Bastards.

The public sector is woefully underfunded. Besides, what chance would some fresh faced young brief have against an establishment law firm. Those city lawyers aren't paid telephone number salaries for nothing. I'm toast either way.

*

As I walk back to the college, the rain starts, and I can feel it soaking through the threadbare strips on my coat. The gate creaks as I enter the college grounds. The back door is now locked so I trudge around to the front, to the reception entrance. It's there I see the tow truck leaving the car park with my beautiful BMW.

In a long yellow pacamac looking like the oversized beach ball she is, the woman form estates helpfully holds the barrier open for the repossession company. I shout after it impotently but the tow truck indicates left, and is gone. The beach ball waddles up to me without a word, hands me a repossession notice then retreats inside, self medicating on a large dose of revenge and retribution.

The grey sky finally gives way to rain, so I turn on my heels and head back into town to get the bus home. My beautiful car is no more. Public transport would be my way of life from now on.

When I get home I'm going to put on my Whitney Houston CD, and take a very deep hot bath. Maybe a few barbituate too.

8 MOTIVATION

'It goes without saying,' says Jenny, the acting Fashion course leader. 'That while you're sharing our office, you should be mindful of the inconvenience you are putting us through.'

According to the building inspector's report, the mezzanine has contributed to an unusual micro-climate within the ceiling void. Mary's spectacular show of strength was in fact, facilitated by a dangerously degraded roof structure. As a result, they've condemned an entire wing of the college.

'And that starts by treating our personal space with respect.'

She heaves the gargantuan potted palm back the four inches I'd moved it in order to create some space to work and it's back in my face. There are eight unoccupied desks in the office, but they're so overrun with photos, pot plants, shoe boxes, fluffy toys and fashion magazines dating back to the middle fucking ages that I'm forced to squeeze my chair under a tiny table in the middle of the room. She re-opens the window that I'd closed five minutes earlier to shut out the noise of building work.

'You will also be expected to contribute to the herbal tea kitty,' she tells me pointing a tin next to the kettle.

With the college's policy of rack-em-and-stack-em, space was tight at the best of times, but now staff and students are all over each other like sewer rats. Tensions are running high; discipline is breaking down.

'And our Children of Africa appeal,' she adds as an after thought, pointing to another tin.

The whole room smells of.. gossip. Woman's hour is on the radio and Jane Garvey is harping on about this year's 'women's power list', and 'women game changers' because it is important to raise the profile of pivotal women in society.. before going on to discuss this season's trend of bubble gum pink jackets.

Fuck sake.

I massage my temples and try to concentrate on the pile of CV's in front of me that are now threatening to take off across the room with the draft from the open window. How the hell can anyone work in conditions like these?

In the emergency reshuffle the Design and Marketing department, i.e Henry and me, were relocated to the Fashion, Hair and Beauty departmental office. Turning back to the latest Facebook or Instagram update on her her IPad, Jenny tells me.

'FYI, promoting moral and social issues through the medium of fashion and beauty is what THIS department is all about.'

Jenny lives in a nice home she calls her 'property' and drives around in Mazda MX-5 she can't afford. She swans around wearing Abercrombie and Fitch, even though she's in her thirties and talks and tweets her friends on the latest IPhone. She paws over catalogues from Victoria's Secret, but says she believes in ethics and equality when in reality she takes whatever shit the sweatshops in Bangladesh and toxic factories in China can churn out for her, facilitated by child labour and the global banking sector.. both of which she strongly disapproves.

It's 'posh coffee' morning apparently, and she takes a sip of her Starbucks, leaving a white moustache of froth on her upper lip that she quickly slurps off before telling me.

'I don't expect being a man with a banking and marketing background you'd really understand ethics.'

The sound card on my laptop gave up the ghost weeks ago, but even so, I plug in my headphones. The bullet point I'm hoping to convey to Jenny is this:

- FYI, STFU

The CV's in front of me are applications for next terms intake. Normally it would be Henry's job, but he's still on sick leave with his perforated eardrum. They're a complete clusterfuck of every CV solecism you could ever muster. It's as if someone Googled 'top CV gaffes you should avoid,' and circulated it as a fucking template. No matter, I've decided to apply asset management techniques as a guiding principal.

An applicant is no different to any other asset, stock, share or commodity you'd consider adding to an investment portfolio with a three-year view.

A few basic rules apply:

- Avoid trading too frequently
- Do not become emotionally attached to an investment
- Stick with your winners, sell your losers
- Past performance of sectors provides the most reliable information about future performance

For 'sector' read 'social group' because past performance of certain social groups are better than others. That's right, if it isn't abundantly clear by now, success in education is all about, discrimination, discrimination, discrimination.

Take the social group, 'working class white boys.' They leave school with far fewer GCSE's than any other group. They are more likely to become a victim of violence, victimisation, suffer depression and commit suicide but are much LESS likely to seek help or support. They are also the group most likely to under perform, fail and drop out of college entirely.

This would put most sensible investors off from the get-go. But if, in a misguided bout of market mentalism, you are tempted to take a punt because maybe you have an under represented sector in your investment portfolio, bear this in mind - they are the least 'hedged' of any sector or social group. Despite under performing all other groups by a large margin, they have the least amount of support - less grants, less subsidies, less scholarships, no government minister to represent them, no social engineered intervention or any representation by special interest groups, lobbyists, the law or even their own families.

In short, they are the under performing, unhedged toxic assets of the education system and it is the reason educationalists and their establishments refuse to invest in them. After all, as an 'educational investor,' you're not running a fucking charity here.

Will you be reprimanded for filing their CV's under 'bin' purely on the basis of social grouping? Will your blatant acts of unequal treatment and discrimination even be questioned?

Get real.

The last and most important point you should consider are 'prevailing market conditions', or 'political climate.' So instead of being investigated for flagrant prejudice you will be lauded by upper management and Ofsted and celebrated for your inclusivity credentials and phenomenal results. A double whammy!

Jenny's phone rings. It's Carol letting her know that she'll be late. Despite being deputy head of department, Carol's desk is located in the Fashion, Hair and Beauty department. Not having her own office, apparently proves her egalitarian credentials. In reality, sharing an office with the girls means she has more opportunity to chat, because I still haven't met anyone who knows what she actually does in this place.

Jenny glances at me with my 'shut the fuck up' headphones on, and thinking I can't hear, decides to switch to loudspeaker so she can multi task talking to Carol with slurping coffee, eating pastries, Tweeting and being late for her students. The conversation goes like this:

```
Carol:   I'm just calling to let you
know I won't be in for 'posh coffee'.
I'll be late again.
```

Carol late? No shit.

Pope.

Catholic.

```
Carol:   Sooorryyy!   I totally forgot
about Garfield's appointment at the
vets this morning.

Jenny:   Oh noooo, poor Garfield, is he
OK?

Carol:   Oh he's fine, he's just
getting neutered.   Routine operation
really.
```

It's scary how easily women talk about such things; as if getting your balls hacked off is akin to having your nails trimmed.

I cross my legs.

```
Jenny:   Do you want me to call HR and
tell them you have a migraine or
backache or something?

Carol:   No need to bother them,
besides, I'll probably be back by
lunchtime.. maybe.   Just wanted you to
know, so you can let someone else have
my coffee.
```

```
Jenny:  Oh that's sooo thoughtful
Carol.  Thank-you.

Carol:  Oh, here's the vet now.

Jenny:  Oh is that the time I'll have
to go too.  OK, well give Garfield a
big snuggle from me.  Byeee!
```

It constantly amazes me how easy it is to throw a sicky in this place. Coming from the private sector - banking in particular, I learned one thing about being ill. You never are, unless of course you're dying. Even then, only if you're dying of something contagious. But throwing a sicky in the public sector is like farting in the midst of all out chemical warfare. It means nothing. Sick leave is 50% higher in the public sector than the private and that's despite the numerous holidays and other benefits to alleviate stress and prevent absenteeism. You'd think someone by now would have spotted the fact that IT'S NOT FUCKING WORKING! Women, it goes without saying, throw more sickies than men. That's without the 'hidden statistics.' Coupled with the long holidays, and a raft of maternity and other statutory paid leave, to be a woman in the public sector is like being on permanent fucking holiday with a big fat pension thrown in for good measure.

Patriarchal society my arse.

On the Radio, Jane Garvey is now having a conversation with the Minister for Women and Equalities lamenting the apparent sexualisation of young women and society's failure to encourage more girls into politics. Girls are apparently aspiring to be too much like the models and actresses they see on TV, and this is plain wrong according the minister.

Jenny bundles up her folders and paraphernalia and hurries from the room to her students, blatantly NOT offering me Carol's coffee that's sat in it's cardboard carrier on her desk going cold.

Bitch.

Back on the radio, the Minister for Women and Equalities is still banging on.

'In my opinion Jane, this media pressure is behind rising levels of depression, anxiety and eating disorders amongst girls.'

She doesn't of course, provide any evidence to back this opinion up, or do a comparative analysis for boys. But this doesn't worry Jane Garvey, because Jane doesn't need evidence to know that females are the real victims here.

As they always are.

'So I have procured the relevant resources, tools and support from Government for my initiative; an initiative aimed at turning girls away from these unrealistic notions of beauty and popularity in the media and instead pointing them in the direction of political and business leadership.'

In other words, the Minister for Women and Equalities fervently believes that girls should aspire to be prime ministers and CEO's of large multi nationals because this is far more realistic and appealing than trying to emulate those attractive, popular, young women in the media who have sexy boyfriends and a Twitter following ten times the size of the minister and Jane Garvey combined. Aspiring to be a frumpy middle aged feminist with a husband ball deep in rent boys, living in a loveless marriage with kids who resent their career obsessed mother will be far more rewarding. And by God she will use as much tax-payers' money as it takes to make girls believe this crap because it's the sort of aspirational pressure that will definitely not lead to inadequacy issues and instead turn them into happy, carefree feminists.

Lol.

Jane Garvey, as always is incensed at the unfairness of it all, so she finishes off her show by stuffing her divorced face with cake that some celebrity chef - a man - baked for her earlier, before telling her listeners that on tomorrow's show, she will be discussing society's cultural fixation with being slim. 'Are we just doing it for men,' she wants to know?

Fuck sake.

I switch the radio off and close the window to shut out the sound of men hard at work, desperately fighting a rear guard battle to shore up the collapsing infrastructure of society. But it's no good; I can't concentrate.

Then a thought occurs to me; an out-of-left-field, carpe diem moment, and I go to Carol's desk and part the domesticating detritus like Mosses parting the Red Sea. I switch on her computer, and when prompted for a password I try common variations around the theme of 'Garfield' none of which work, until 'Garfield2014', and that's it, I'm into her account.

I crack my knuckles, take a sip of her coffee and begin.

First I head to the auto correct feature in Word and Outlook so 'Carol' auto corrects to 'Jeremy Clarkson,' 'learners' corrects to 'minions' and 'college' corrects to 'death star'. Next I change the regional and language settings in the control panel to Romanian. Moving over to the auto hotkey settings I make the 'g' the caps lock key and 'h' the space bar. I sit back, take another sip of coffee and survey my handiwork.

I'm tempted to do more – so I do.

While I've still got Word and Outlook open I go to the dictionary and replace some select words with misspellings. 'Feminist' becomes 'feminazi', Comic Sans becomes Wingdings and finally I call reception and tell them she's not at her desk, so could they page her over the PA. A minute later, the entire college is wondering; Why's Carol not at work?

With my work done, I check her browser history and flinch. It's a long, long list of Internet dating sites, cat rescue centres and God forbid, sperm donor clinics.

I really wish I hadn't looked.

I close her computer down feeling somewhat nauseated and move back to my laptop and find two emails in my in tray. Another departmental meeting has been scheduled - in the library this time and one from an old flame and colleague - Svetlana, wanting to meet up for a drink.

And most probably sex.

Which would be a very, very bad idea.

No trust me.

It would.

9 NEEDS OF THE ORGANISATION

I've got solicitors letters stuffed in my drawers. I've got debt collection notices stuck to my fridge. I've got county court judgments pinned to the fucking corkboard. I'm so desperate for a proper job with real money that I've actually thrown my first ever sicky, and agreed to meet up with Svetlana. Like Miles, Svetlana is blissfully unaware of my employment status. As she sips her Chardonnay at the Sofitel hotel bar at Gatwick, I spin her my well-rehearsed yarn about the contract in Dubai that this damned non-disclosure agreement prevents me from discussing with her. I'm hoping Svetlana can get me back into the game.

Here's a girl who just a few short years ago would have lapped the sweaty dick cheese off anyone that could get her a job in marketing. She did, and I gave her that job. I've only got myself to blame for the demise of that firm. These days Svetlana is deputy head of European development for a major marketing company. Her social network is like a who's who of the entire industry and her client list reads like a Tolstoy novel.

In short, the tables have turned.

In short, Svetlana matters.

Gatwick is like Svetlana's second home; I'm not entirely sure where her first even is. Like many of her Eastern European compatriots, she is a work machine. It's no wonder annexing Poland was top of Hitler's European agenda. Don't talk to me about glass ceilings and inequality in the work place. Here is a living example of how any woman, given a healthy work ethic, good looks and a tight little body, can gobble her way to the very top of any greasy pole.

I'm drinking scotch. The only reason I drink it is because she thinks it's the height of sophistication. But let's be honest, it just tastes like fucking battery acid to anyone who wasn't brought up in a European backwater on a diet of deep fried farm waste. It's no surprise it was invented in fucking Scotland.

The important bullet points you should be making on Svetlana are these:

- She's blonde, 29 and about a size 8
- She's 5'6ish with great skin and bone structure
- She drives an Audi RS7 Sportback with an Ice Silver Side-blade finish and all the extras
- She loves rough sex

And when I say rough sex, I mean, not so much in a deviant sense, more something the legal profession might refer to as, 'sexual misadventure' or 'on the grounds of diminished responsibility.' Svetlana doesn't do rough sex. She owns it. If cage fighting and sex ever homogenised into an Olympic sport, Svetlana would be an overnight sensation. Her idiosyncratic taste in the bedroom department probably explains her otherwise unlikely engagement to the local Tory MEP. The engagement however, doesn't stop her from calling to let me know about a four hour stopover between flights and I have to start wondering, once again, whether having the living crap beaten out of me is a price worth paying to maintain a valued network of key contacts. LinkedIn remains strangely silent on the subject.

Today she's wearing a new tailored Stella McCartney, light wool, short skirt suit in charcoal grey and carrying a tan, hand stitched mulberry attaché case.

'So,' I tell her, casually steering the conversation towards a job. 'I'm thinking of a return to the UK. I've got a few offers in the pipeline from head-hunters, but I'm looking for something a bit more challenging.'

I leave the statement open for her to fill with a list of contacts, but she seems more interested in playing with my BMW key-fob, which I still retain, despite my beautiful car being repossessed.

'Carl!' she scolds. 'You letting yourself go!'

The fuck?!

Despite my public sector job, I still keep myself in great shape, even though my gym membership has now run out and maintain a full head of L'Oreal Paris Men Expert Excell 5i, trimmed that very morning. I'm also wearing the Gresham and Blake suit that I bought with my severance pay.

What the suit says about me is this:

- I'm smart, but not uptight.
- Relaxed, creative and fun without compromising style.
- I have definitely NOT let myself go.

'You still got facking BMW ?! I give you my Audi dealer number. Brand up, fack sake!'

I shake my head cooly, telling her, 'sentimental value,' and take another sip of the rancid scotch. It doesn't stop her from writing down the number and pushing it into my top pocket anyway. I would have rented a new bloody Porsche for the day and parked it at the entrance for her to see, but that would be stretching the budget way too far. Instead I had to share the shuttle bus from the airport with a load of chavs on their way to Magaluf.

Fuck sake.

I tell her about Miles's party invite, more to keep the conversation away from sex than any real social reason and surprisingly she agrees to come. She also drops something in my drink that I watch dissolve with some trepidation.

'For later,' she winks.

And I'm hoping to God, that whatever it is has been cut with plenty of pain-killers. She slides a surreptitious finger through the buttons of my flies and slowly, expertly rubs my cock to attention.

A tap on my shoulder makes me turn around to...

'Jeremy! What the hell are you doing here?'

Jeremy beams at me like he's just found a long lost puppy.

'Carl! I wasn't expecting you to be here either. We could have shared a lift.'

I blink at him. I have no idea what he's talking about or why he's here. Svetlana, never missing a networking opportunity, removes her hand from my cock and thrusts it over my shoulder at Jeremy, telling him simply 'Svetlana Symanski.'

He shakes her hand, still warm from my cock. Too weird.

'Jeremy here is our er.. Equality and Diversity.. advisor,' I tell Svetlana, hoping to God he doesn't mention the college.

'So are you here for the AoC conference too?' he asks Svetlana.

Her smile remains fixed and she looks at me baffled.

'You know, the Equality and Diversity event?' he prompts. 'There's an awful lot on body dysmorphia this year isn't there?' he adds, desperately trying to move the conversation along.

There's another pause, then Svetlana slaps me hard on the shoulder.

'Dat is vat job secrecy is all about?' she asks.

Now I have no idea what she's talking about, and I'm starting to wonder whether the scotch/sex drug cocktail is taking effect already. My boner is certainly staying resolutely in place. I tap my nose and wink at her, drain the scotch from my glass and grimace. Frankly I can't think of anything else to add so I order another Scotch. She places a palm on her forehead remembering some marketing statistics.

'Da, body dysmorphia. Two and half billion euro market. Self harming big too; growth market, customer retention, brand loyalty,' she says, suddenly looking at me impressed.

I put a finger to my lips, look around the bar then lean in close.

'It's all very hush-hush,' I whisper.

Jeremy's the one looking confused now so he asks her.

'You seem very informed on the subject Svetlana, are you a surgeon or something?'

There's another pause, then Svetlana spits her chardonnay across the bar and starts honking hysterically.

'Da, Da.. I surgeon! Doct-tor Svetlana Symanski! HA HA! Hallo Doct-tor Svetlana Symanski! HA HA!'

I take the opportunity to take Jeremy by the arm and lead him away from the bar, ordering Svetlana another Chardonnay as I leave in the hope it will shut her up.

'Jeremy. Dr.. Symanski and I are discussing some.. delicate issues concerning.. er..'

'Body dysmorphia?' he offers.

'That's right,' I confirm.

Jeremy glances over at Svetlana sceptically.

'Yeah, she's a little.. unconventional I'll grant you, but one of the best in her field,' I reassure him.

I lead him further away from Svetlana's honking hysteria. Jeremy looks at me, puts a hand to his chest and gives me a concerned look.

'Of course Carl, if you need some privacy but,' he adds, touching me lightly on the shoulder. 'I am a qualified councillor if you need to.. discuss anything personal. There are a lot of rogue surgeons around, particularly from Eastern Europe.'

I nod sagely at him and pat him on the arm.

'Thanks, but I'm OK Jeremy. I just need some time alone with Svet.. with Dr Symanski.'

More howls of laughter from the bar. Jeremy takes a last look at Svetlana, waggles his fingers at me shyly and mercifully exits the bar. I straighten my jacket and take a deep breath.

When I sit back down. Svetlana is dabbing her eyes with a paper coaster. She tugs at the cuffs of her jacket. Down to business.

'So, what you vont?' she asks. 'We go to restaurant, get something to eat - maybe coffee. Or..'

She grabs my lapel and jerks me in close, waggling her room card at me
'We go upstairs to fack?'

She glances at the clock above the bar and answers what was evidently a rhetorical question anyway.

'Da, we fack.'

*

Before we're even in the hotel room, she slams me against the wall of the corridor. Despite her slight frame, her brute strength knocks the wind out of me, and my gasps for air are mistaken for passion. Her tongue starts pounding my mouth like a hammer drill. In the military, it's known as 'shock and awe'; incapacitate the enemy by scaring the living crap out them. It's not like I didn't know what to expect. I've been here before.

I've only got myself to blame.

Without missing a tongue stroke she swipes the card on the door and kicks it open. I don't think in the natural order of things I should be manhandled into a room by a woman, any woman, particularly one that's barely three quarters' my size. But in a blur of pain and fear, I am being fucking brutalised here. Trying to squeeze a conversation in about job prospects in an increasingly competitive marketplace, seems increasingly unlikely, as I try and construct strategies to survive the onslaught. It's around about now I wish I hadn't ducked out of those CPD safeguarding courses Carol was always banging on about.

Staggering backwards, I trip over my own feet, fall to the ground, catching my head on the corner of the bed.

When I come too, my hands are tied and Svetlana's sex drug has taken effect. You could knock walls through with the cock on me, and the world is playing out like some Jan Svankmajer film; like some horrific stop frame animation.

```
SCENE 01

FADE IN

--INT. HOTEL BEDROOM - DAY--

OVERHEAD:  Carl is lying face up naked
on the floor.  His arms are tied
beneath him.

CUT TO:

CARL'S POV:  On top is Svetlana also
naked, riding his limp body like a
horsewoman of the apocalypse,
screaming expletives at his terrified
face.

CUT TO:

EXTREME CLOSE UP:  A string of butt
beads is forced into Carl's anus by
the manicured, ringed finger of
Svetlana.

PULL BACK:  Carl writhes violently,
much to the obvious approval of
Svetlana.

CARL
Use some fucking lube!  Use some
fucking lube!
```

CUT TO:

OVERHEAD: Carl, his back slamming against the headboard, now wearing a gag. Svetlana attempts to shatter his pelvis with her arse.

CARL
(Muffled expletives)

CUT TO:

CARL'S POV: Carl lying face up on the bed with Svetlana pinning him down.

CLOSE IN: Svetlana's hand grabs the bottle of champagne from the ice bucket by the bed.

PULL BACK: Svetlana sits up and pours the champagne over her naked breasts.

SVETLANA
'Leek dem bitch slut, Leek my titties!'

CARL
(DISTRESSED) 'My hands are tied and I've got beads up my arse!'

CUT TO:

OVERHEAD: Svetlana throws away the empty bottle. It shatters against the wall.

CLOSE IN: Svetlana slaps Carl hard across the face.

SVETLANA
'Leek dem Carl, you facking whore!'
She does it again, and again...

And again...

FADE OUT

TIME LAPSE

FADE IN

--INT. HOTEL BATHROOM - DAY--

OVERHEAD: Carl is doubled over, lying face down in an empty bath, handcuffed to the groin ring of a full body cock harness.

CLOSE IN: Svetlana firmly grips the protruding butt bead handle with both hands.

SLOW MOTION

CARL
'No.....'

Svetlana pulls hard, and the butt beads pop out one by one, but snag on the back of the cock harness, snapping the stainless steel ring into a set of scalpel sharp pincers. And the rest... the rest is silence.

FADE OUT

SCENE 02

FADE IN

--INT. HOTEL RECEPTION - DAY--

MONTAGE - CARL LEAVING HOTEL ON PARAMEDIC TROLLEY

-- Carl being pushed at speed on a trolley towards revolving doors.

-- A trail of blood leading from the lift to the trolley

-- The sheet covering Carl catches on the revolving door snatching it away from the trolley.

-- Horrified expressions on the faces of the onlookers on seeing Carl's ball sack in ribbons.

-- Horrified expressions on the face of Jeremy, the Equality and Diversity Officer from Carl's work, who follows him into the ambulance.

FADE OUT.

END

10 INITIAL, DIAGNOSTIC ASSESSMENT

On the wall behind her desk there's an empowerment poster by the World Professional Association for Transgender Health. There's a million ways I could deface it, but I have been advised against any form of 'unnecessary stimulation.' I think the surgeon's euphemism referred to masturbation but I'm not taking any chances.

At the hotel, before the ambulance arrived, Svetlana cleared up the scene faster than a mafia hit man. When the paramedics found me I was sat in the empty bath, tears in my eyes, half unconscious with my ball sack in my hand, just as she had arranged me before calling the ambulance. And once again I am left to ponder on her proficient talent for this sort of thing, and how it dovetails into a loving relationship with her MEP boyfriend.

No matter.

Me keeping Svetlana's name out of the whole thing means this:

- Svetlana owes me
- And she knows it

Despite copious amounts of analgesic, the pain in my lone, surviving testicle prevents me from sitting still for more than a few seconds. I shift uncomfortably in my seat, taking care not to dislodge the catheter. My Gresham and Blake suit has given way to a t-shirt and sweatpants after being cut away by the surgeon. Bloody heathen. Brogues have given away to soft soled trainers. Anything to cushion the impact of anything else on my delicate, stitched scrotum.

The bullet points you should be making about the woman talking to me are these:

- She's wearing ethnic jewellery and a yak's wool sustainable sourced cardigan - which stinks of cats
- She must be in her mid 40's if she's a day and unlikely to cause any unnecessary stimulation
- She drives a six year old, red, Kia Rio
- She has badly self applied dyed hair which gives the appearance of a mange variant
- She is my assigned psychiatric assessor and an 'x' in the wrong box from her can have me sectioned for life.

I know this type, but I've got it covered. Flirt too much and she'll think I'm some sexual predator. Don't flirt enough and she'll take offence; think I don't fancy her and am making aspersions on her defunct femininity. It's a fine line I know, so I've cracked a few jokes to lighten the mood and also to show her I'm relaxed and not suicidal and in need of sectioning under the mental fucking health act, which is what these things are ultimately all about. I don't think she's really buying into the jokes though. I have a box of Oxycodone in my pocket from the doctor and it's another hour before I'm supposed to take the next one but the pain is creeping up on me again.

The thing about psychoanalysis is this: It fucks with your head. So much so that it is proven that in the wrong hands, it can actually create major psychiatric disorders in people who initially have only minor psychosis. It's called the 'iatrogenic effect,' and it's a bit like an electrician attempting to change a fuse in your consumer unit with a hammer drill, then telling you the problem goes way deeper than he first thought. The most notorious examples of this are false memory syndrome and multi personality disorder when, after years of therapy and bizarre court cases involving testimony by 'expert' psychoanalysts, they discovered that neither condition actually existed in patients until they underwent psychotherapy. That's right, like the Tyrell corporation, these fuck-wits had actually retrofitted patients with entirely false histories and personalities.

What's more, talking therapies such as cognitive behavioural therapy are not that effective on men anyway, because guess what? Men don't particularly like chatting with middle-aged hippy munters because guess what again? We're not women! Once you're on that psychotherapy treadmill however, it's like the Eagles said, 'You can check out any time you like, but you can never leave.' Like any quack enterprise, psychotherapy relies on customer loyalty programs and repeat business, so once you've been diagnosed, your name ends up on NHS equivalent of a PPI insurance database, and the tenacious fuckers will never, ever leave you alone. Especially when you are your psychotherapist's favourite diagnosis.

So at times like these, it pays to remain focused.

By concentrating on her disastrous hair, I can temporarily alleviate the pain in my groin, although I then have difficulty focusing on what's being said. And I really need to pay close attention for the reasons I've just outlined. Hair. Pain. Conversation. Like some chicken, fox, grain game to get to the other side of the session.

'And now Carl,' she says, after an hour of skirting around the subject she's been itching to get on to.

'Do you know about gender identity Disorder and are you comfortable talking about it?'

And here is it is. Her favourite diagnosis.

'Yes,' I tell her, although I'm not entirely sure which question I'm answering.

She scribbles something in her notes. She's on to her fifth sheet already.

'Do you suffer from any other medical conditions. Mental health issues for instance?'

'No.'

Pain, pain, hair.

'Do you ever dress in clothing deemed appropriate to the other gender?'

Pain, hair, pain, pain.

'Ye.. er, no!'

Pause. Look. Pause. Scribble.

'Do you have feelings of identification with the opposite gender?'

Pain, hair, pain, hair, pain, pain, PAIN. I grimace which she takes to be an answer and eagerly marks another box on her clipboard.

'Would you say you are comfortable with your own assigned sex?'

'Yes! I'm comfortable!..'

Raising my voice in this way pulls at my catheter, it's only slight, but the pain is immense. I fling my head back, bite my lip and whimper like a baby. Again she takes this to be an answer and scribbles something in her notes.

She shifts her chair closer while I blink back tears of pain. Slowly I move to the other buttock, as much to alleviate the scrotum pain as get away from the approaching hair. She takes my hand in hers and tells me.

'Your case is not unique Carl. Acute onset of gender identity disorder can often lead to a strong desire to.. remove the genitals, as you know. There's no shame in what you did or how you feel.'

'I haven't got any fucking 'disorder'!' I bleat pathetically through the tears of pain.

She pats my hand.

'I agree entirely Carl. Gender identity is merely a Western social construct, not a 'disorder.' Sex may be a biological binary, but gender is a whole spectrum of colour. In fact I'm in the process of updating our literature to 'gender dysphoria,' which is far less demeaning. But it takes time. We still haven't updated them from the last name change yet.'

She points a pen over her shoulder at the poster on the wall.

'We're working hard to de-pathologise the condition, but in these unenlightened times I have to work within a recognised terminological framework for diagnostic purposes. I hope you understand.'

I'm feeling claustrophobic and panic starts to set in, and once again I try to plunder the murky depths of education theory to help me out. Watkins advice in times of confrontation is:

'Do not to react to the emotion of the moment. It can be counterproductive.'

His advice is to work through:

- Feel
- Think
- Do

Educational theory; useless as ever in the real fucking world.

I look around the room for other ideas while phrases like, 'reassignment', 'gender incongruence', 'hormonal treatment,' and 'transgender transition surgery,' jump out at me. I randomly twitch my head through a grey mist of pain and nausea, all the time she's marking more boxes; filling in more and more sheets until finally, mercifully she decides to end the session.

'I can see this is causing you some distress Carl so perhaps we'll end it here for now and pick up again, on..' she glances at her diary. 'Next Thursday perhaps?'

As if.

I nod, and she squeezes my hand emphatically doing 'support.'

'One last thing,' she says, picking a bottle of pills from her desk and shaking it at me. 'This is herbal Vitex. It's normally used for feminine hormonal problems, but it's also great for suppressing libido in men. You may want to consider it while you're, you know.. healing.'

She nods at my groin.

'However, if you do find yourself in a situation where you're becoming, let's say.. involuntarily aroused, it may help to adopt none sexual thought patterns. Think of something you find slightly repellent. I have one patient whose pet hates are sea-food and dog mess, so he imagines a dog defecating on fruit de mer. Disgusting as it may sound, he swears by it,' she tells me brightly.

Silence.

I blink, once, twice. Did she really just say that? Did she really put a thought in my head that involved a dog squatting over a plate of French cuisine? I love French food. I did love French food. I feel suddenly nauseous. I have literally nothing to say to this woman.

She squeezes my hand one last time before releasing it.

'I think it'd be OK to discharge you first thing in the morning, once the catheter's removed, but don't be worried. I'm here to support you through this difficult journey. I want you to promise that if you get any urges to.. self medicate again, you will call me immediately. I'm not just your therapist, Carl,' she informs me, dropping to a whispered hiss. 'I'm your friend.'

*

FAO: Hospital Administrator Sussex County Hospital

Re: Mr Carl Waxman - Psychiatric Notes

Identifying Information:

The patient, Carl Waxman is a 35 year old, white male of medium build and average height. He was born in Croydon, Greater London on October 3 1978.

I examined the patient Mr Carl Waxman at Sussex County Hospital for the purpose of psychiatric evaluation. The patient was accompanied in the ambulance by a work colleague - Mr Jeremy Howard, who provided a useful witness statement referenced in this report. The patient cried a little during psychiatric evaluation but appeared lucid. He remained guarded as to the circumstances surrounding his admission to hospital, which he referred to as 'his little accident.'

The patient denied feeling depressed. He was orientated in

all three spheres. Apart from the incident, his memory for immediate, recent and remote events was good, his judgement clear. The patient was, on the whole, cooperative during psychiatric evaluation, looking slightly younger than his stated age, well groomed given the circumstances and responded to questioning coherently.

Chief Complaint:

The patient arrived unconscious at A&E by ambulance, following an incident at the Sofitel hotel at Gatwick. He was admitted to hospital with severe testicular trauma, which resulted in emergency surgery and full amputation of his left testicle. Paramedic and witness statements allude to the fact he was under the influence of drugs and alcohol which toxicology reports later confirmed. A witness statement provided by a work colleague - Mr Jeremy Howard, who accompanied the patient, testified to the fact that the patient may have engaged the services of an unregistered Eastern European surgeon who attempted orchiectomy (removal of the testicles) unsuccessfully, before calling an ambulance.

The patient continued to complain of pain and some memory loss surrounding the incident.

History of present illness:

No record.

Psychiatric History:

There is no history of mental illness, epilepsy, depression, suicide or divorce in the family. The patient denies a history of any neurological disorder insisting he is. 'No mentalist.' He did however seem slightly preoccupied with the idea of sex and admitted to some sexual disorders, saying, 'let's just say, I've had a few in my time.' He declined to elaborate on this, claiming it as 'just my little joke.'

Personal and Social History:

The patient was the second of two siblings and was raised by his biological parents who now live abroad. He reported considerable emotional conflict with his elder brother during his formative years and no longer has any contact. He graduated from Lancaster University in 1999 with a marketing degree. Thereafter, he had several jobs in the second hand car trade before securing a lucrative full time position within the sales and marketing arm of an investment bank. The work environment was competitive with an alpha-male centric philosophy. The patient reports turning to 'putang, chang and Dom Perign-ang,' a reference perhaps to the crutches of sex, drugs and alcohol, during this difficult period in his life; a form of self-medication on which he relies to this day.

He has never been married nor claims to have had any long term relationship. He vehemently denied any homosexual tendencies insisting, 'just because I like my freedom doesn't make me a pillow biter!' He was keen to inform me, that he had a girlfriend once with 'special needs' for which he says, 'I was more than capable of fulfilling,' Although he again claimed this was a joke, perhaps evidence he is suppressing a more caring feminine side to his nature.

Medical History:

There is no record of any other medical conditions.

Criminal History:

There is no record of a criminal history.

Mental Status Check:

The patient is fully orientated.

Precipitants:

The patient's competitive male-centric home environment and later his male-centric work environment precipitated an affected alpha-male, pseudo-persona perhaps contrary to his repressed 'feminine' nature.

Cross-Sectional View of Current Cognitions and Behaviours:

This alpha-male, pseudo-persona has perhaps forced the patient to repress his true gender identity and the witness statement provided by his work colleague, allude to the fact that he engaged the services of an unregistered, gender reassignment surgeon to re-balance his gender equilibrium which backs up this hypothesis.

Diagnosis:

- Gender identity disorder
- Drug and alcohol abuse.

Prognosis:

With six weekly sessions of gender based, cognitive behavioural therapy (CBT) and guidance on legitimate gender reassignment options; the patient could make an informed and healthy decision on his future course of action surrounding gender reassignment. I have also recommended a limited use of Vitex as an anaphrodisiac and discussed arousal suppressant techniques, until the patient's injuries are more fully healed.

Conclusion:

It is my belief that the patient is safe to return to the community under his own care, with a firm recommendation that he be placed under my personal psychiatric observation and CBT (as the county's foremost authority on gender identity) to help him express and come to terms with what he obviously feels is an embarrassing 'disorder.'

Catherine Cohen. BA (Hons), BABC

11 POINTS OF REFERRAL

In the morning, Svetlana is waiting to pick me up as arranged; parked across two ambulance bays in her Audi RS7. With its Ice Silver Side-blade finish glinting in the sun like that; it's beautiful. Even the Oxycodone doesn't remove the pain of envy. Today Svetlana is wearing a Donna Karan Fluid Stretch Suit with a Tissue Satin Bodysuit. It's stunning. For good measure, I pop two Vitex that the psychiatrist said would keep potentially agonising erections at bay, and wash it down with a small bottle of Evian.

I've had plenty of time to rehearse my 'chat' with Svetlana during my brief stay in hospital. Through the awkward police interviews, through the painful surgical procedures, through the compulsory psychiatric evaluations, I've been working through ways of turning this to my advantage. Re-assessing my life plan. Losing a ball can do that to a man.

I'll tell her this:

By not returning to Dubai as planned, I've missed a pivotal

meeting, resulting in losing a crucial account for my employer. Because of this; because of her, I now have to look for another job, a new job, but on the same telephone number salary I was on before to - you know, keep me in the same lifestyle I have became accustomed. That's the guilt card. Playing from a position of 'victim' is a new tactic for me, but it seems to work for every fucker else in society so why not give it a try? Besides, sometimes you have to play the cards dealt to you.

If this doesn't work I still have an ace up my sleeve. I'll tell her that journalists are sniffing around. Money has been offered. Big money. I hate to threaten the political career of her MEP fiancé, but hey what can I do? Business is business. Without a job I need the money. I'm sure, you of all people Svetlana, will understand?

It's beautiful. It's simple. It can't fail.

She looks me up and down.

'I pick you up!' she tells me rhetorically, like somehow this makes up for everything.

'Yes,' I observe. Pause. 'Thanks.'

Her eyes settle on my sweat pants. With the surgeon cutting up my beautiful Gresham and Blake suit I had to plunder these clothes from the lost property box. The trainers are two sizes too big, like big clown shoes and the left and right are different brands.

'How is balls and vinky?'

'They're.. recovering thanks,' I tell her.

She leans back. Takes in the full picture as I get in the car beside her and says.

'I take you home.'

I've been shaved with disposable hospital razors, I stink of surgical wipes and my hair hasn't seen a professional stylist in nearly two weeks. The Nike sweatpants I'm wearing look almost sacrilegious against the black, hand stitched leather of the Audi's interior.

The Michelin Pilot Super Sports tires screech as she pulls out of A&E into the path of an approaching ambulance.

'You look like sheet,' she observes.

Then that laugh again.

Not a nervous laugh. Not a guilty embarrassed laugh but a full on belly laugh like the whole thing really is the funniest fucking thing she's ever seen.

'Ha, ha.. you look like leetle hobbo! Leetle tramp with floppy vinky!'

Her hysterical and uncontrollable honking tells me two things:

- The guilt card is probably a non-starter.
- As a little girl, she probably used live kittens as footballs.

'Finished?' I ask her.

She nods, wiping away tears of laughter, but still unable to stop.

'It's something the newspapers might call a 'human interest story with a political twist' don't you think?'

It's like someone capped the air inlet on her honking engine. She looks at me, reaches down and pulls a Kleenex from a little stainless steel Muji box near the handbrake.

'You know what reporters are like?' I tell her regretfully, in case the message hasn't quite sunk in. 'Waving their wallets around; looking for a good story, and well...'

'You no need vorry about journalist,' she interrupts, dabbing the underside of her eyes with the white Kleenex.

'Bartek take care of journalist.'

She thumbs the back seat and I turn to look.

'Preeviot!' booms Bartek.

'Christ!' I shout back, nearly pissing my sweatpants.

Bartek's jacket is almost identical to the seat leather, and he has a shaved head as wide as the head-rest. It's no wonder I didn't notice him. He's like some Audi optional extra.

'Bartek is.. lawyer,' Svetlana informs me.

Bartek smiles proudly showing his gold capped teeth.

'I lawyer. I tell people what law is,' he confirms, leaning forward and patting a shovel like hand on my shoulder, adding, 'Sorry to hear about.. balls and vinky.'

Which only sets Svetlana off honking again. Bartek doesn't

laugh. He just leaves a hand on my shoulder and gives me a meaningful look which tells me two things:

- He's a man and understands testicular trauma isn't a laughing matter
- He probably knows more about testicular trauma than is comfortable to know

As we drive, I pop another Oxycodone. What the hell? Where do I go from here? Svetlana takes the pill box from my hand and peers at it in disgust before throwing it onto my lap, which makes me wince like someone flicked a lit cigarette at my crotch. She digs about in her Hermes Kelly bag at her feet and pulls out several small bags of powder, peers at them before handing them to me.

'Dis make you feel like 'He Man' again,' she informs me.

It dawns on me that free bags of an indeterminate sex-drug cocktail are about as much as I'm going to get out of this situation. Defeated, emasculated, depressed, I feel like the last clown left at the circus, when the laughter has died, the bailiffs have been, but still, I'm being slapped around my big goofy clown face with a giant, inflatable banana. Slap, slap, slap. I'm not sure how much more humiliation I can take.

'I tinking about your friend - man at hotel,' she says, twirling a hand around in the air trying to remember his name.

'Jeremy?!' I offer.

'Da, Jeremy. He make me tink about employment law; about equality-diversity.'

'You've been thinking about workers rights? Really?'

Svetlana hands me a solicitor's letter addressed to one of her Russian clients. The words 'anxiety,' 'distress,' 'alarm,' 'insult' and 'compensation' are highlighted in green marker.

'What is meaning of dees,' she asks, stabbing at the highlighted words with red talon like nails.

I skim through it quickly. I've become somewhat of an expert of solicitor's letters of late.

'It looks like a claim for unfair dismissal,' I tell her. 'A big claim. Your client is going to need a good solicitor.'

'Solicitor pwah! Bartek, he go to house and talk to employee about, how you say - out of court settlement?'

Bartek laughs and kisses the walnut like knuckles on both fists and I'm starting to think the pair could make an excellent contribution to the college's Business Communication course.

'But situation is not easy. Bosses turning organisation into legitimate business, dey vorry about litigation, unfair dismissal yadda, yadda. Dey ask me, 'Svetlana, give me insurance against such tings', but no such ting; no such insurance product possible!'

'Er yeah, I don't think you can insure yourself against law breaking. Don't you have any legal contacts?' I ask her.

'I dip toes in lots of pies,' she tells me. 'Bosses from Russia, Ukraine, Poland, Slav's, Czech Republic, dey tell me, Svetlana what is this equality-diversity ting, I no understand! If worker is lazy sheet you tell them 'go!' But I tell them not here, not in dis country. Here, you give sheet workers human-civil rights and plenty money. It crazy!'

She twirls a finger at her temple.

'What happen in dis country?' interrupts Bartek shaking his head at me.

'Your Winston Churchill, he spit in eye of Hitler; your Margaret Thatcher she fight Argentina, crush unions and stamp on Europe, but now, psst.. now your Prime Minister, no like hurting feelings of leetle homosexuals. He is..'

Whatever word he is looking for is lost in that great, bear head of his. He asks Svetlana something in foreign and she tells him, 'pussy.'

'Da, he is big PUSSY!' barks Bartek.

Not only do I have my ball ripped off by a lunatic Polish psycho, I'm now expected to defend the state of British domestic politics against an unhinged Stalinist! It's like the cold fucking war all over again.

'He's not exactly Putin, I'll give you that,' I agree half arsed.

'Putin, ha! He crazy also.'

Make up your mind you schizoid Cossack.

'I need consultant on equality-diversity,' Svetlana tells me.

'You give me number of this.. Jeremy, then I maybe help you find new job.'

I hesitate, but my wriggle room is somewhat limited here so

I tell her I'll text it to her later when I've recharged my phone (and figured out how to monetize the situation). In truth I don't even have it. Why the fuck would I have Jeremy's number on my phone anyway?

Svetlana drops me off at home but I decide against inviting her in, especially with Bartek in tow. What's true for politics, is also true for social etiquette - never let the fucking Russians in, because as sure as eggs is eggs, in no time at all you're knee deep in empty vodka bottles, Kalashnikoffs and tanks and when you ask them politely to leave they spike your tea with polonium-210, annex your bathroom, cut off the gas and threaten your entire block with nuclear Armageddon.

*

Back at home I run the bath while wading through the mail; all the usual crap about final reminders, debt collection, store cards and other letters threatening to drop kick me in the face. Like the CV's, I file them under 'bin'. I put Melvin Bragg on the radio and position my laptop on the sponge rack across the bath and settle down, very slowly, into a deep soapy relax and a game of Amnesia: A machine for pigs. Granted not the safest way to play a computer game that scares the living crap out of you at every turn, but it's a risk / pleasure balance that I'm willing to take at this juncture.

I'm just getting into it, when the news comes on and there's a report about two Russian oligarchs slugging it out in the high court. According to the news-reader, the case has already generated legal costs of around £100m. It's estimated that one of the silks alone, bagged somewhere between £3m - £10m. With all this Russian money washing about, why would Svetlana want to piss about with Jeremy?

What possible interest could the Wolverine of Londongrad and her mafia/oligarch clientele have with equality and diversity? Are they really that scared of our liberal legal system that they would want to hedge against it when they've got the likes of Bartek to help with any legal and personnel issues? I'm missing something big here - I know it. But whatever happens, she's not getting Jeremy's number. If she finds out I've been working at a college for the past few years, that's it; it'll be instant Coventry.

Forty minutes in and the water is getting cold, so I put my laptop to one side, have a wash and inspect the sad void that was once my left nut and can't help feeling a great sense of loss. The coagulated blood around the stitches dissolves into the bath water in tiny, pink rivulets. My cock however remains undeterred and stares up at me with a look in it's eye that says, 'Please.. spank me.'

Ahh, how could I say no?

A few short minutes of tentative pole waxing later, my eyes begin to close.. then:

BAM!

There it is.

A dog taking a fucking great dump on French food. The more I try to ignore it, the sharper the image becomes and to make matters worse, Jane Garvey is now on the radio banging on with another twist on the same old narrative, that all men are bastards and women are victims of a patriarchal society.

Ad nausea.

Slowly, slowly it grows obvious that my offering to the god of lonely men is just not going to happen. Fuck. Bitch. Cunt.

..and Fuck.

I raise myself irritably from the filth of the bath water and step directly onto my laptop, splintering the screen and keyboard. I jump around on one foot, picking out plastic splinters from the other, attempting to upgrade my swearing, but seriously, where do you go from fuck, bitch, cunt?

'Knob-head!' I shout at the shattered mess.

The power light flickers before dimming and finally shuffling off its mortal coil.

Jane Garvey is now interviewing some gold digger, who's bitching about her thirty-five million divorce settlement.

'Thirty-five million sounds a lot, but I just know he has some other fortune stashed away offshore somewhere Jane, which is why I am suing him for more. This whole thing is very distressing for the children but I'm not doing this for the money or myself, I'm doing it out of a sense of justice, fairness and for other women in my position.'

Jane of course, is lapping it up as she always does. Justice and fairness.

Fuck sake.

Here's another nobody, who has done nothing more than say 'I do' at the altar and is now making a very lucrative living out of victimhood, shouting her shortcomings and indignation from the roof tops and pocketing the compensation payments procured for her by opportunistic lawyers using laws invented in a time when women weren't even expected to work for a living.

I take a fistful of painkillers, encase my ball sack in a fresh dressing and wrap myself in my Paul Smith bathrobe. I turn off the two squealing harpies on the radio and stream Wolf of Wall Street to the TV.

```
[Let me give you some legal advice:
Shut the fuck up!]
```

12 EQUALITY AND DIVERSITY

Rachel likes Abba and is into retro furniture. In short, she's a 'seventies kinda gal'. This she tells me over dinner at some swanky French restaurant, the name of which I failed to register when her mother told me to be there.

Of course when in the late 70's girls were interviewed regarding their aspirations in life, they put 'love and marriage' as their top priorities in life with 'career' at the bottom. The late 70's also peaked as the era that enjoyed the best quality of life as indicated in the Genuine Progress Indicator (GPI).

Over the following decades, 'career' slowly moved to the top of the list of girls top priorities and 'love and marriage' moved to the bottom. During the same period the GPI showed a marked decline in the quality of life and happiness for the entire nation.

Coincidence?

I think not - here's a chart to prove it:

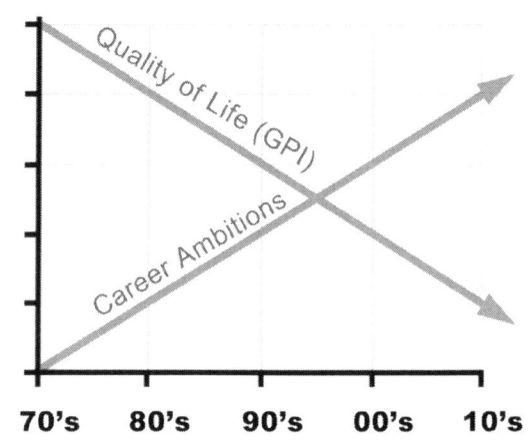

Quality of Life (GPI)

Career Ambitions

70's   80's   90's   00's   10's

In short, being a 'seventies kinda gal,' means Rachel's priorities in life are 'love and marriage.'

I assure the waiter that there's nothing wrong with my seafood platter as he takes it away untouched; I'm just not that hungry for some reason.

Fucking psychiatrists.

Rachel's mother gets off the phone to her husband as dessert arrives.

'Ernie, sends his apologies Carl,' she tells me. ('Do call me Bethany') 'He's been working late, but will be joining us for coffee very soon.'

No shit, I bet he's gutted he missed out on this evenings little soiree.

'I do hope you and Ernie can patch things up Carl. I think a little apology about the erm.. the unfortunate incident, wouldn't go amiss when he arrives.. hmm?'

I listen and nod. I eat and drink more wine then listen and nod again. It's one of those restaurants with crisp white tablecloths that serve tiny portions on plates the size of drain covers; the type I used to frequent when I had a proper job and didn't think twice about the expense.

For the purpose of this exercise I've decided to go along with the idea of dating Rachel, thinking, perhaps there may be an upside to all this. There'd be regular sex obviously, which wouldn't be so bad and rich parents are always a bonus. Although the daughters of rich parents tend to have expensive tastes and expect everything to be paid for by other people. And when I say other people I mean men, so maybe that isn't such a good prospect.

On the other hand Rachel's mother seems to get off on the fact I'm not working in the financial sector, so perhaps she'd agree to a little 'allowance' to date her daughter in the style she's no doubt become accustomed to. Then after a week or two of excessive, unrestrained, early relationship sex and expensive meals at exotic locations, I'll fake a brain aneurysm or something and act kinda retarded until she suggests a 'trial separation.'

Or perhaps I could go in the other direction and go all aloof and show no interest in her at all. Although women do go ga-ga over that sort of shit and fill your answer phone with whiny messages like, 'what have I done wrong,' and 'tell me how I can change,' which is frankly nauseating and embarrassing, especially when they turn up at work or on your doorstep in the middle of night threatening to kill themselves and waking up all the bloody neighbours.

I'm not having that again.

Rachel's mother ('How many times Carl? Call me, Bethany!') pinches Rachel's cheek, smiles and sighs again for about the tenth time that evening.

'Oh, just look at you two love birds. You remind me of Ernie and I at the start of our relationship. Back then I was a model and Ernie had just started at Lehman Brothers.'

And I'm thinking yeah, but I bet he wasn't dating you with a shotgun held to his head. Rachel smiles coyly at her mother then at me. She reaches across and squeezes my hand.

'I'm so glad you called, Carl. Daddy scared you away before we had chance to exchange numbers. He can be such a brute sometimes; I was very cross with him. Mummy's quite the detective isn't she?'

Detective doesn't quite cut it Rachel. If you ever wake up to find yourself as an involuntary guest in a secluded mountain cabin with the smell of boiling bunny in the air, Rachel's mother would be the one standing at the bottom of your bed taking a fucking great sledgehammer to your feet.

'She is.. she certainly is. Do you often bring your mother on dates with you?'

'Oh, that's such a crude term, don't you think Carl?' Rachel's mother interjects. 'In my day, we didn't go for 'dating' or 'co-habitation' or even 'long engagements.' We just stepped right up to the altar and made it work.'

The word 'altar' brings to mind pedestals on which live sacrifices are made. No amount of matrimonial 'spin' will ever change that fact.

'Erm.. made what work?' I ask, putting my spoon down slowly.

'Marriage Carl!'

Fuck me I think I'm about to have a coronary.

[Lieutenant, bomb that tree line about 100 yards back! Give me some room to breathe!]

'Oh mother, I think it's a bit premature to be thinking along those lines,' says Rachel.

Damned right it is. But I can see it; I can see it in Rachel's eyes, already she's got the dress picked out. She knows the typeface she'll be using on the invitations and how many gluten free canapés will be needed.

'Marriage?!'

I've never blurted in my life, but I do it now.

'Calm down dear. I know you young people like your so-called 'freedom,' but you don't stay young forever and there's nothing worse than having children when you're too old to run around after them, believe me.'

'Children?!'

I've blurted again. I've multiple blurted within seconds; I should write to a fucking woman's magazine about the experience. Marriage and children are words that conjure up images of a Russian Gulag; a trudge from church to morgue via B&Q and Mothercare through a bleak, Siberian winter. This cannot be happening.

'You can't be serious? I can't do that.. Bethany. I just can't,' I plead with her.

'Oh I know some of those awful modern comedians compare marriage to a long prison sentence, but it's nothing like that in reality. Besides, given the choice I know which I'd rather choose.. ha ha, hmm?'

'I.. !'

I've got nothing left in me. I'm spent. She passes me her handkerchief while looking around in embarrassment.

'Don't be such a crybaby Carl and get a grip. Marriage isn't so bad once you're used to it. As long as you put the effort in and don't spend seven days a week chasing the bloody financial markets. That's the wonderful thing about you Carl; about being a college lecturer, it means you'll have plenty of time to spend with your wife and children.'

As if by some creepy coincidence the lounge version of Whitney's 'Greatest Love' starts playing gently in the background, like some scene from 'American Psycho,' just before the victims are brutally dismembered.

'You know, until you have your own children, you don't realise what a blessing they really are. They instil one with the hope that it's not too late to better ourselves,' she says, looking into the regency framed mirror on the wall and patting down her hair.

'Money is all well and good, but it's family that matters. Children are our future Carl, I firmly believe that.'

It's fucking creepy is what it is. She beckons the waiter over to order more wine, then starts humming along to Whitney. It's like being kidnapped by a mother and daughter Stepford wives combo. I can only hope she concludes her thought process in the same way as Whitney Houston when musing on the thought of the future and children - with barbiturates and a hot deep bath.

'Oh mother, you're so.. incorrigible,' says Rachel blushing.

```
[There's mines over there, there's
mines over there, and watch out those
goddamn monkeys bite]
```

The secret is to stay calm, although why it has to remain a secret I've got no idea. Rachel's mother continues to bang on about our future plans.

'I'm thinking perhaps a country house wedding would be nice, with pictures taken in the grounds and then perhaps a honeymoon in the Maldives, with maybe a stopover in Singapore - you know, for the shopping, then a house in the home counties. I've been looking at the Oftsed reports of schools..'

I feel like some back seat passenger in a Thelma and Louise movie, as the car hurtles towards the Grand Canyon, kicking up a cloud of dust in the face of the pursuing police; a clown passenger with big fucking shoes that are stuck under the seat so I can't move; can't jump - and a smile; yes a smile, a painted fake smile on my face, presenting an expression of jocularity to the world, when really I'm petrified and crying inside - crying and singing a heartfelt aria like some tragic character in an Italian opera, just before the wheels leave the ground. It'd have to be a mixed media production obviously.

This wine just isn't hacking it; I need more drugs; hard drugs.

'Daddy!' says Rachel, seeing Ernie Weiner approaching the table.

He orders a large scotch before his coat is even off.

'Sorry I'm late, darlings,' he says, air kissing his wife's cheek and smiling at his daughter. 'Problems at work.'

He waits for the scotch to arrive and takes a long slug before he can bring himself to look at me

'So this must be Carl?' he says, with that expression only a father can give; an expression that broadcasts to the room, I'm a convivial sort of guy and welcoming this young fella into the fold, while conveying to the 'boyfriend', a fervent desire to take him out the back and decorate his face with a baseball bat for defiling his cherished daughter. 'The boyfriend.'

He emphasises the 'd' in 'boyfriend.'

'Carl has something to say to you, haven't you Carl?'

Rachel's mother, raises her eyebrows at me in a meaningful way while sipping her wine.

'Yes. Mr Weiner, I'm sorry about the erm.. unfortunate incident the other week. It was crass and..'

'..and you're obviously prepared to pay for the damage,' he concludes.

Thankfully Rachel's mother steps up to the mark.

'Ernie don't be ridiculous, Carl can't afford a Ming vase on his wage!'

She looks at me and gives me a wink and I'm thinking, maybe she isn't such a complete psycho after all. Perhaps a generous allowance for dating her daughter may well be on the cards.

'How about Carl just pays for this meal and we'll hear no more about it?'

'Yes of course, it's the least I can do.'

You've got to be kidding me!

I've only got one card left to max out: I'm financially fucked and can barely afford the bus fare home.

'Well then, that's that. Rachel and I are just off to powder our noses, and discuss.. plans.'

She winks at me again and holds out her hand to Rachel, like she's taking some six year old to the toilet.

'In the meantime, now that the air has been cleared, perhaps you two boys can start afresh.'

We watch them go. Now I'm racking my brains for a subject to discuss with the legendary Ernie Weiner. As soon as they're out of earshot he leans in close with a fatherly smile and American bon ami.

'Listen here you limey bastard,' he says; face pulsing shades of red and purple. 'I know your little game. Miles told me about you wanting a job; he said you were working in Dubai and now I find out you're just,' he struggles to find the words to express his disgust. 'Public.. sector.'

Ouch!

He stops and drains the rest of his scotch and does a little shiver, and I'm thinking Miles actually came through for me despite being a pissed cunt. Nice one.

'If you think by dating my daughter I'm going to lift so much as a goddamn finger to help you find a real job, then you're mistaken dipshit. You might have charmed my wife around your little finger but if I hear she has given you so much as a dime of my money you motherfucker, I will personally see to it that your life is a living breathing hell of the highest magnitude.'

Americans. Happy with school massacres and calling everyone 'Motherfucker,' (which is really disgusting when you think about it,) but mention the word 'toilet' and they have a fucking seizure. However within the vitriol and hatred: within the thinly veiled death threats and flecks of spittle, I think I see a glimmer of hope and perhaps a solution to this whole omnishambles.

'Mr Weiner, sir. There's no other way of telling you this other than coming straight out with it, so I will.'

I take a deep breath.

'Your wife is blackmailing me with false allegations of rape and threatening me with legal action unless I marry Rachel. I'll be honest; I haven't got the means or resources to fight her. She's making wedding plans as we speak and Rachel is going along with it.'

I pause for some reaction, but there's none so I press on.

'Mr Weiner, sir. Rachel is a lovely girl; really she is fantastic and will make some lucky man very, very happy one day. But I'm no more ready for this type of commitment than you are to have me as a son-in-law. So perhaps you can have a word with her and you won't ever have to see me again.'

He stares at me expressionless. I'm not sure he has even registered what I'm saying. Then he does a kind of throat cough, like he's choking on an ice cube or something. Still expressionless. Another throat cough, and suddenly I'm wishing I hadn't skipped the First-Aid-At-Work CPD training then I might know what a Heimlich Maneuver is all about. Then finally it comes out. Not an ice cube, but a laugh. He sits back in his chair and starts banging the table, eyes wet with tears that bring disapproving stares from the neighbouring tables.

'What's so funny?' I ask him. 'I'm serious!'

This only spurs him on to a heightened state of hilarity. There's a brief lull when he leans forward and puts a heavy hand on my shoulder and tells me.

'Welcome to the club kid.'

And he's off again. He's still laughing five minutes later when Rachel returns with her mother.

'Well,' says Rachel's mother frowning. 'I can see you two boys have hit it off.'

Coffee is served and Ernie Weiner, brings himself to some sort of manageable equilibrium, save for the occasional aftershock and wiping his eyes with his napkin. I have no idea if this is a good thing or a bad thing, and again I'm on the back foot resorting to just listening, nodding and drinking like some social gimp.

*

Later in the car park, Ernie Weiner sidles up to me and we fall into step behind the two women just out of earshot. He puts a companionable hand around my shoulder.

'Hey kid,' he whispers, even though I'm thirty fucking five. 'What food puts a woman off sex for life?'

'I don't know, what?' I ask miserably, and he starts that throat-coughing thing again that passes for a pre-laugh.

'Her wedding cake!'

And he's off again.

'And just for the record kid,' he says once he's calmed down again. 'When my wife gets an idea into her head, she don't let nothin' stand in her way. And I mean nothin'!'

He slaps my back so hard it completely knocks the wind out of me.

'So you're on your own with this one kid. I ain't gonna help. But if you ever make my daughter unhappy,' he adds, starting to laugh again, then stops, sighs and whispers. 'I'll get my people to peel off your skin with a blunt knife and use as it as a condom to butt fuck your mother. Do you understand me?'

Creative. Scary, but creative.

Ernie Weiner waves down a black cab and Rachel comes over and kisses me on the cheek.

'This was fun wasn't it? Call me next week,' she tells me, before climbing into the back of the cab with her psycho parents.

So no sex either.

Happy families.

13 INCLUSIVE LEARNING

I've purchased a Putnums Deluxe orthopaedic cushion that the finance department inform me is a claimable expense. The less balls you have it seems, the more the public purse strings loosen for your convenience and comfort.

This is no news to me.

The catheter might have long gone, but the pain steadfastly remains, so I'm popping Oxycodone like they're going out of fashion. I settle down to catch up on yet another score of email memos from Carol; a reminder not to use the word 'fail' as it can be demoralising to learners, it's 'referred.' And it's not 'learners' anymore, it's 'stakeholders.' A reminder not to use red pens when assessing work as it can be deemed 'offensive.' That's right, an offensive pen colour. It takes a seriously slow work day, even by education standards to come up with shit-for-brain policies like these. I wasn't even aware that people used pens any more. There's no restrictions on printing ink so I fill in an IT order form for more red ink cartridges. My next set of assessment will be awash with red printed feedback, but most definitely not in Comic Sans.

When our civilisation sinks, as it surely must for the sake of evolution and the survival of the species, there'll just be a slick of deadwood and memos. Archaeologists in years to come will sift through the digital debris to find clues to explain the sudden collapse of our culture, and there it'll be, a memo not to offend 'stakeholders' by failing them or giving feedback in red pen.

Sparta eat your heart out.

I'm in the middle of preparing a PhotoShop module in which learners are required to airbrush the pubic hairs and tattoos from lingerie models as part of a fashion magazine makeover. Just the thought of it necessitates more Vitex and Oxycodone but I could have saved myself the bother, because Carol comes into the office being trailed by the twelve year old IT technician with greasy hair carrying a replacement computer. She stops and looks me up and down with undisguised distain, her eyes momentarily resting on my baggy sweat pants. I shrug and tell her.

'I had a little accident.'

'Which would explain your absence from the safe guarding course again I presume?' she snaps.

I shrug my shoulders regretfully.

'I'm on to you Carl,' she says, spittle jumping from her painted red lips and arching it's way onto my laptop.

I look down at it with over exaggerated disgust but she's undaunted.

'I know what your extra curricula activities involve; your relations with stakeholders, ignoring memos, sabotaging my computer and general laissez-faire attitude to this job.'

I put my hand to my chest the way Jeremy does when he's shocked or offended.

'I'm shocked and offended,' I tell her, looking at the IT kid.

The IT kid, knees bending under the strain of a moderately heavy, re-conditioned computer, looks away pretending not to listen.

'My student feedback and results are always excellent, and my assessment and 'inclusive' records are amongst the best in this college.'

Her fists are pumping, pumping in sync with her ovaries.

'Bastards like you Carl!' she says, before gathering herself and lowering her voice. 'Bastards like you, always slip up eventually. I'm gathering evidence on you and I'm going to see you up before a disciplinary hearing very soon, I promise you.'

She wags a finger in my face then storms over to her desk with the IT kid struggling in her wake. I give the bird to her back. I can't be in the same room as Carol, not with a boner. It wouldn't be right.

Pearls before swine.

I need a pick-me-up so I take out a sachet of 'He-Man' gifted to me by Svetlana at the hospital and make my way to the disabled toilets on the first floor, which are never used. They are never used because an access ramp leading to the accessibility lift was laid at an incline of 1:09 instead of 1:12. This made it a health and safety hazard and so the lift was deemed out of bounds. Over £150,000 worth of equipment out of the college budget, wasted for the sake of two inches of concrete - which if added to the access ramp would contravene planning regulations, as it would interfere with access to an adjoining fire door - which if removed would contravene fire regulations.

You couldn't make this shit up.

It would have been cheaper and easier to employ some lacky to stand by the stairs, whose sole job would be shove PHaTs and cripples up and down the stairs in Evac-chairs. What sick fuck invented Evac-chairs anyway? It's like some multi disciplinary sport involving origami, the skeleton run and building infernos. What could possibly go wrong? The training video alone takes half a day to watch and reminds the untrained dickweeds it expects to use these death traps to:

'Never let go of the Evac-chair!'

No shit, really? I'm glad you mentioned that.

I say the disabled toilet is never used but that is something of an exaggeration. With it's inaccessibility to the disabled, hygienic wipe clean materials, sturdy grab rails, non slip floor, generous leg room, low lying mirrors, sink, pan, coke friendly ceramic surfaces and clean towels within easy clutching distance, it makes the ideal sex gym. It even has an emergency pull cord in the event you were to say, find yourself locked in with someone with the sexual voracity of Svetlana, and in need of emergency backup. It's like a bunch of sex addicted mentalists were given free reign at an art and design therapy session to come up with their dream room and miraculously ended up drafting the first plans for disabled toilets.

Design awards have been handed out for less.

Besides, the disabled don't even use public toilets. They're all at home hiding under their beds trying to avoid Atos assessors.

Come on, you've read the papers.

I set out two lines on the cistern and greedily toot them both. Five minutes later I'm striding down the corridor pain free, on top of the world and master of the universe.

```
[- How're you feeling, Jimmy?
 - Like a mean motherfucker, sir!]
```

Two minutes after that, whatever was in Svetlana's ketamine, coke cocktail mix is reacting horribly with my Vitex and Oxycodone. My head starts to rage with all sorts of psychedelic crap. Walls start to pulse; the floor undulates. Ten meters from the office door and I'm holding onto the wall like the last piss head out of the pub. So close, but it might as well be an ocean to cross. I'm a small kid on a bouncy castle again, grasping at the flimsy walls crying my frikin eyes out to make it stop, while the big kids, spurred on by my pleas for clemency, bounce even harder to make the thing jerk and roll even more. I'm petrified.

When it comes down to it, kids are all evil little bastards.

Then if that wasn't enough, oh God, the boner starts. Svetlana again, no doubt cutting in some fast acting Viagra. Doubled over in pain I lean against the wall for support, face and palm sliding along the wall, dislodging an anti drug poster and taking it with me. My sweatpants begin to tent pole and I half goose step, half slide my way forwards, or backwards, it's hard to tell which. It's like a cinematographic mashup of 'Being John Malcovich' and the fucking 'Shining'.

```
SCENE 01 - CCTV Footage

FADE IN

--INT. COLLEGE CORRIDOR - DAY--
OVERHEAD CCTV: Carl crawls his way
along the wall towards an office door

CUT TO:

INTERSECTING CORRIDOR: Hilary - Hair
and Beauty Tutor - approaches,
clutching make-up bag.

EXTREME CLOSE UP: Carl's face, beaded
with sweat and in extreme distress,
looks down at his boner.

HILARY PERSPECTIVE: Looks down to see
Carls boner too.

CLOSE UP: Hilary freezes and clutches
bag even closer.

PULL BACK: Legs apart, Carl launches
himself from the wall and staggers
like a drunken marionette towards
Hilary, preceded by the large erection
mouthing the words. 'HELP ME!'
```

CUT TO:

OVERHEAD CCTV: Carls hand reaches out to grab hold of Hilary. Accidentally swipes the bag from her grasp while the other hand grapples with her breasts for support.

CLOSE UP: Hilary draws a four inch healed stiletto back.

CLOSE UP: SLOW MOTION

CARL
'No.....'

PULL BACK: Hilary kicks Carl square in the nut sack. Carl falls to the ground in incredible fucking agony like you wouldn't believe, blood stain appearing at the crotch of his sweat pants.

CUT TO:

--INT. COLLEGE RECEPTION - DAY--

MONTAGE - CARL LEAVING COLLEGE ON PARAMEDIC TROLLEY

-- Carl being pushed at speed on a trolley towards revolving doors.

-- A trail of blood leading from the doors to the trolley

```
-- The sheet covering Carl catches on
the revolving door snatching it away
from the trolley.

-- Horrified expressions on the faces
of the students on seeing Carl's nut
sack, again torn to ribbons.

-- Horrified expressions on the face
of Jeremy, the Equality and Diversity
Officer from Carl's work. Racing to
escort him in the ambulance. Again.

FADE OUT.
```

*

FAO: Hospital Administrator Sussex County Hospital

Re: Mr Carl Waxman - Psychiatric Notes # 2

I again examined the patient Carl Waxman at Sussex County Hospital for the purpose of psychiatric evaluation, having arriving conscious at A&E for a second time accompanied by the same work colleague as before - Mr Jeremy Howard (perhaps more than just a colleague?). I also drew on the material supplied to me by social services and my previous psychiatric observations relating to the patient for the purpose of this report - see attached documentation.

Witness statements allude to the fact the patient was again under the influence of drugs which toxicology reports confirmed - see attached document. Witness statements also suggest he had also been uncharacteristically 'unkempt', although he denies being depressed or having any suicidal ideation.

He was mostly orientated in all three spheres. His memory for immediate, recent and remote events was this time vague although his judgement was still good. In contrast to the previous psychiatric observation, the patient was less cooperative and looked his stated age, despite it being approximately a week between observations, perhaps indicating a depressive state.

Chief Complaint:

The patient was admitted to hospital via A&E following an altercation with a female colleague in which he allegedly committed a sexual assault. A kick to the groin by the alleged victim repelled this 'attack' resulting in his admission to hospital. He complained of severe pain, and some memory loss with minor perceptual delusions.

History of present illness:

The patient had previously arrived unconscious at A&E with severe testicular trauma, as a result of a failed attempt at orchiectomy (removal of the testicles) by an unregistered surgeon. A toxicology report at the time also showed a cocktail of alcohol and drugs. As a result, one testicle had to be removed by surgery. My psychiatric diagnosis at the time was acute onset of gender identity disorder - GID (Now officially referred to as 'gender dysphoria' - Yay!), leading the patient to turn to extreme means of self-medication. Cognitive behavioural therapy (a recommendation made from the previous psychiatric report) had not yet fully begun.

Psychiatric History:

See previous report.

Personal and Social History:

See previous report. In addition, although the client still vehemently denies homosexual tendencies, I am inclined to believe the work colleague who accompanied the patient in the ambulance - Mr Jeremy Howard, maybe more than just a 'colleague' as the patient insists.

Medical History:

No record of any previous medical conditions.

Criminal History:

There is no record of a criminal history prior to this incident.

Mental Status Check:

The patient was partially orientated with slightly depressed mood. The recent attack was provoked, in my opinion, by a form of self-harm by proxy, and directed at a part of the body the patient considers alien to his repressed identity. Again my diagnosis is a recurrence of acute onset of gender dysphoria - GD, in addition to others - see below. The toxicology report again shows drug use, which the patient claims were for pain relief.

Precipitants:

See previous report.

Diagnosis:

- Gender dysphoria. (NB referred to as 'gender identity disorder' in previous report)
- Drug and alcohol abuse
- Mixed sexual deviation. (In men with satyriasis we usually see an excessive constant preoccupation with the desire for coitus).

Prognosis:

Taking into account the latest incident, the patient would benefit from a more extensive (twice weekly) intervention of gender based, cognitive behavioural therapy (CBT). This should be reinforced with fortnightly sessions of Ecotherapy. I have also prescribed Priadel as a mood suppressant in addition to recommending higher doses of Vitex to be used at the patient's discretion. He has also agreed to drug and alcohol counselling. With this in mind, the patient should make some progress towards the challenging route of transition.

Conclusion:

The patient struggles to appreciate his primary diagnosis - gender dysphoria, and therefore perhaps failed to recognise the 'self-harming' symptoms when they present themselves. This was greatly exacerbated by an unfortunate interaction of prescribed and illegal drugs resulting from his secondary diagnosis - drug and alcohol abuse. His tertiary diagnosis of mixed sexual deviation, could also have been a contributing factor.

It is therefore my belief that the new prescription and the apparent determination of the patient to enter alcohol and drug rehabilitation, will enable him to conduct himself in manner that will present a minimum danger to himself or other people, until full treatment is under way. It is my recommendation that he should be returned to the community, albeit under closer, psychiatric observation and social services intervention.

Any further relapse should be considered a sign that the patient is not stabilising or heading in the direction of recovery and more drastic intervention should be considered.

Catherine Cohen. BA (Hons), BABC

14 SCHEMES OF WORK AND SESSION PLANS

In addition to my Putnums Deluxe orthopaedic cushion, the college have also paid for an orthopaedic chair, keyboard and a Kensington SoleMate foot-rest with anti skid platform. I do however, have my one remaining battered and bruised nut mercifully intact, so I'm still obligated to leave the comfort of my orthopaedic props to do some work.

Migraines and ovulation are as yet, skiving options not available to me.

Henry is still milking his fucking earache and remains absent. It means I get to pick up the slack by taking two classes at once. Luckily, his students are well versed in tutor absenteeism and in an overwhelming show of sympathy and solidarity pissed off at the earliest opportunity leaving only two of them to join in with my class of twelve. That's about a 70% attendance, a statistic most departments in the college would give their right nut for. I use the term 'attendance' loosely, because about half are either texting, tweeting or checking Facebook on their phones; some are in the library 'researching' and the rest are moving cursors around a screen to no apparent purpose.

I'm talking to Ben, assessing the progress of his communication design module. I wouldn't say Ben is fat, but he's probably only ever played a football game from between the goal posts. He is also the son of a local millionaire paper merchant. Against my better judgement I accepted Ben's transfer onto the course because I reasoned there may be a chance of discounted printing costs from his Dad, but the thing about self made millionaires, is they're self made millionaires for a reason - they're all tight cunts. So I'm stuck with this feckless kid to no apparent advantage to anyone. He still hasn't put pen to paper or decided what he wants to do after a fortnight of racking his brains so I ask him to list his interests.

After giving it a lot of thought he lists his interests as these:

- Cooking (because he takes high calorific ingredients from the fridge and piles it on ready made pizza bases)
- Grand Theft Auto V.

It would be a complete waste of time asking this retard to correlate these interests into any sort of innovative, motivational or even coherent idea, so I tell him to design decal graphics for a GTA V vehicle, promoting pizzas to the in game demographic.

As simple as this sounds, it'll be shit. Ben's work is always shit and nowhere close to the standard you'd expect at degree level. Problem is, if I fail Ben I'd have to fail half the class and that would severely disrupt the college's pass rates. Failing a student is never an option. Ever. Even if they never show their face in class, there's a host of re-sit, deferral, transferral and appeal opportunities which are designed to keep the college's pass rate at somewhere near acceptable levels. Added to this the endless dumbing down, differentiation, behind the scenes interference and general malaise, the value of qualifications are virtually impossible to determine.

Qualifications these days are like the convoluted financial toxic assets that led to the market meltdown of 2007. And like the Financial Standards Authority Inspectorate, who turned a blind eye to the warning signs, the Ofsted inspectorate turn a blind eye to declining standards and shit work, allowing the problem to snow ball until finally it wipes out an entire nation at the bottom of the hill in an pedagogical crap-ocolypse, leaving the tax payer to pick up the bill, and the inspectorate to pick up their public sector pensions from a safe distance.

I talk to Maria next. In the words of the mother superior from the Sound of Music, when I'm with Maria I'm 'confused, out of focus and bemused', which considering this is a communication design module, she's looking at a first. The similarities with her namesake however end there. This Maria is no gold digging, singing nun deserting her fellow countrymen by fleeing Nazi occupation with her millionaire sugar daddy. No, she's a card carrying Spanish box bumper with a very slight hygiene problem.

This is her pitch.

She wants to do a thesis on mass groupings, from riots to flash mobs and study their effectiveness as a means of communication by analysing key words from twitter traffic both before and after the event.

Keep up.

By doing this she will demonstrate the most effective form of mass group communication method to promote or conversely demote issues being raised. Using this thesis she hopes to possibly go on to get a job in public relations organising smart mobs for promotional companies.

She's no looker this girl, but if I was still in a position to do so, by God I'd give her a job on the spot without any oral leverage whatsoever. Maybe this feminism thing is rubbing off on me.

'I want to start with sthee Slut Walk in a-Brighton next week,' she tells me, in her Kitty Softpaws accent which leaves me feeling very conflicted.

'Well you've got to start somewhere,' I tell her, which I'm aware, makes no sense whatsoever.

'Iss opportunity for to open my eyes todally to the filling of anger of sthee weemen and analyse sthee twitter traffic.'

She closes her eyes and takes a deep intake of breath. What she imagines smelling in a crowd of half dressed, radical feminists, I can only guess.

'You know what I mean Mr Waxman?' she asks me, as I nod emphatically.

'I do. I so do Maria. The oppression of women is an important issue to be..'

'No!' she shouts, grasping my knee with a grip of iron, which makes me jump out of the seat. 'Iss important to detach from sthee issue, and jus to asezz objectively sthee key words in the twitter traffic.'

I can't teach this girl anything. She's an unstoppable force of nature and my work here is done. I'm not sure it ever started, if the truth be told

The whole SlutWalk phenomenon of course has been accredited to the Canadian feminist movement, but credit where credit's due, it has it's roots firmly in the British tradition, 'the walk of shame.' whereby, in the early hours of the morning, red faced, British women sneak home en masse through the towns and cities of this great nation in a state of half dress, stilettos in hand and carrying a deep sense of remorse, having been sump pumped sober by some scrawny doozer in a flea bitten bedsit. It takes North Americans however to give it a re-branding and turn it into something all together more affirmative and bring it out into the light of day.

As the Canadians have demonstrated, British women shouldn't be ashamed of such things. Us Brits should take pride in traditionally meaningless, alcohol-fuelled hedonistic cultural dynamics that have given the world more than just sluts. We have given it football hooliganism, binge drinking and boy bands that survive to this day, despite being subjected to unceasing attack by socialist/progressivist thinking.

I reluctantly turn my attention to the rest of the students, the 90% who in all honesty will be in a bun fight for shelf stacking jobs at Lidl following graduation if they're lucky.

I take a deep breath.

I know what's coming.

Nearly all will claim various self-diagnosed acute learning difficulties and 'special circumstances' as mitigating reasons for doing fuck all work. Learning difficulties and special circumstances that mean I'm expected to differentiate my delivery, support and assessment for each and every last one of the lazy cunts, tripling my workload to get half the results. I say 'expected,' but all I do in reality is just tweak pre-written, banal platitudinal shite from previous assessments and bang it out as feedback. I find online bullshit generators are more than adequate for this exercise in futility. No-body reads this crap anyway.

So ubiquitous is the appetite for complicating and medicalising the human condition that education will jump on any reason to lower expectations and excuse laziness or 'motivational deficiency' to explain their failure to educate to any sort of decent international standard. We're a hairs breadth from introducing crystal therapy to align the chakras of 'stakeholders' because their chart shows Capricorn rising, necessitating help from central government for 'special' alternative needs, because pastoral support in this area is woefully underfunded, which explains the declining standards.

Or to put it another way.

Yes it's all shit, but you can't blame us educationalists, it's because British kids are just plain dumb and way more mentally retarded than foreign kids! I don't know; maybe they have a point. But does all this intervention make them employable?

Does it bollocks.

They wouldn't last two minutes in the real world, with some

wank-bag shouting at their face to get the job done twice as quick on half the budget: when they realise they're not a 'valued team player' or 'colleague,' but an expendable 'employee.' And no you can't go and cry to the pastoral support officer because the real world hasn't got a fucking clue what that is, so get off Facebook and get over yourself you whining pussy and do the work you're paid to do.

Unless they go work in the public sector.

In which case, fill your boots.

Just saying.

I sit next to Chantelle-Jo. I don't need to bullet point Chantelle-Jo, just imagine what a 'Chantelle-Jo' would be like and you'll be spot on. Chewing on her gold loop earrings she tells me she was listening to my conversation with Maria and feels 'inspired.'

Bloody hell, a three syllable word.

Someone's been eating their super fruits.

I'm thinking, this could go either way. She tells me she wants to scrap her original idea of posters promoting a local nightclub, and now wants to promote 'woman's rights.'

Here we go.

'Aha. So what have you got in mind?' I ask with excruciating sincerity.

'Maybe design a poster for that SlutWalk Maria was talking about to promote women's rights to - you know, places where girls can't go to school. Like that Pakistani girl what got shot by the Taliban in Korea.'

Korea? Genius. And like Jeremy, this girl thinks the only form of mass communication is posters. I nod thoughtfully at Chantelle-Jo like I'm seriously giving a toss, and then in an attempt to get her to think outside the box for a second, tell her.

'Why posters Chantelle-Jo? Perhaps you could just invite Malala Yousafzai on the SlutWalk with you to promote the issues you want to raise.'

As much as teaching is like pushing shit up a hill sometimes, there's some fun to be had in fucking with young impressionable minds, as I'm sure the Islamic preacher Abu Qatada or Anjem Choudary could attest. At the end of the day these guys were probably just fucking about and having a laugh.

'Who's Masala Yousaf?' Chantelle-Jo asks.

'Ma-sa-la is a curry Chantelle-J. It's 'Ma-la-la Yousafzai. That Pakistani girl 'what' got shot by the Taliban,' I tell her.

'Cool!' she says looking wistfully into the distance, as if getting shot by the Taliban is some celebrity right of passage.

'And we could like, wear headscarfs and stuff?'

'Maybe with fake blood?' I offer.

'Hijab!' shouts Casey from across the room, pointing to a Wikipedia page. 'The headscarfs are called like.. 'Hijabs' and they look sooo cool.'

The key to political engagement of youth it seems, is to 'accessorise'

'What they for anyways?' asks Chantelle-Jo.

'Iss worn in zee presence of men for modesty,' replies Maria, looking up from her work.

This causes deep creases to furrow in the orange foundation of Chantelle-Jo's brow.

'Mo-des-ty?' says Chantelle-Jo, tasting this alien word. 'Wot, like to stop men fancying them and stuff?'

'Si,' confirms Maria.

'Is they like.. lesbians?' asks Chantelle-Jo, still grappling with the concept of modesty.

'No, they prefer to rely on the allure of their voice,' I tell Chantelle-Jo. 'Just like you do.'

'This is awesomest idea!' Maria butts in. 'It is, how you say, la yuxtaposicion?'

'Juxtaposition,' I correct.

'Si, la yuxtaposicion of sthee clothing freedoms of womens!'

Why can't I just keep my mouth shut? Chantelle-Jo and Casey beam at Maria, like a molecular connection has taken place. Chantelle-Jo feels emboldened.

'We could all do it!' well, not you Carl obviously' - you're like, a man.'

The girls giggle at the thought of me being 'like, a man.'

'Yeah, you know what?' I say looking at my watch and thinking if this thing takes wing, certain people may take exception to seeing my students dressed as Hijab wearing SLUTS. 'I wasn't serious. Maybe you should stick to the nightclub idea.'

'But it's an awesome idea!' says Chantelle-Jo, echoing Maria with uncharacteristic resolve, as if reassuring me in my moment of doubt. 'I'm gonna tweet wassername like you said.. Masala, and ask her.'

'It's Ma-la-la. Maybe we should talk about this during contact time Chantelle-Jo,' I suggest, slightly worried now.

Casey gives me a suspicious look.

'You don't need to talk about it!' she tells Chantelle-Jo. 'I'm up for it if you are. It'll be mental!'

'Me also!' says Maria.

This thing is starting to take on a life of its own, so I don't say another word. I just put my trust in apathy. It's usually the one constant I can rely on in an ever-changing world.

'Sorted,' says Chantelle-Jo standing up. 'I'm going to the Fashion department for some headscarf material. Who's up for it?'

Maria, Casey and two other girls stand up. I nod my head and off they trot to the Fashion department via the canteen where they'll hopefully stop for a coffee and diet doughnut and talk about inconsequential crap and reset their brains to 'standby' and forget the whole fucking conversation ever took place.

Besides, the Fashion department gives nothing away. Not because they're millionaires, but because if there's one place where talentless, hysterical, bitter artists and painters end up, it's education.

Which is dangerous.

Nobody needs a history lesson to remind them of the incomprehensible atrocities, frustrated painters are capable of committing and the unprecedented revulsion it causes. You may well ask, how do such people receive sufficient popular support and how can we learn from history to ensure such vileness never happens again? What is it about human nature that makes the monstrous evil of Hitler and Tracy Emin possible in the first place?

Think on.

15 DIFFERENTIATION

Word on the departmental grapevine is that Dr Jones will be announcing his retirement at the meeting this morning. Because of the lack of rooms, the meeting is to be held in a cordoned off section of the library at 11:00am, presumably to allow any overrun to eat into lunchtime instead of teaching time. It's taken the old fart nearly four decades to finally wise up to the fact that meetings never run to schedule. Maybe in the good old days, but not now.

Go figure.

Enter Carol and her attack dogs from the Fashion, Hair and Beauty departments at 11:08am sharp. The look in their eyes tells me they have the scent of blood in their noses after their pre-meeting, meeting. Karen, arrived earlier and is already asleep and mercifully in the carrycot beside her, so is her baby. Henry has returned to work, but still traumatized from the assault resulting from the last meeting, he's sat as far away from Karen as it's possible to get in such a confined space. He never pressed charges because after all, as Carol told him, it was all just a 'silly misunderstanding.'

As Fashion, Hair and Beauty settle down with banal, inconsequential prattling, the student reps begin fingering their phones, preparing themselves for yet another session of in-depth disengagement.

'Before the meeting begins, I'd just like to put some rumours to rest,' says Dr Jones irritably, catching everyone off guard with his forthright interruption of the ceremonial pre-meeting chatter.

Jeremy and the fat, ugly woman from estates suddenly jostle their notes.

'There has been some.. conjecture that I am planning to retire in the near future. Where this rumour began I have no idea but for the record, I'd like to state here and now that there is no truth in this gossip and I plan to be around for some considerable time yet!'

Never listen to gossip. Absolutely, goddamn right.

Carol, denied the opportunity of her traditional territorial pissing exercise by addressing the meetings first, is visibly taken aback. She has been positioning herself for the old boys job for as long as anyone can remember. This was to be her moment.

'But it's all over the department. Everyone was expecting you to announce it today!' she protests, like somehow expectation equates to reality.

'I'm sorry to disappoint you Carol, but you shouldn't put any credence in gossip. As Socrates said, 'Strong minds discuss ideas, average minds discuss events, weak minds discuss people."

Carol's jaw drops theatrically.

'Are you implying that the entire department is of a weak mind Dr Jones?'

'What? I didn't imply that at all,' he protests.

'Because we may not all have 'doctorates,' she says, bunny fingering the word angrily. 'But we have a right to discuss our own opinions without being insulted!'

'I didn't mean.. of course you have a right to your own opinions Carol, but not your own facts, and on this occasion the fact is I'm not retiring so my job is not up for grabs!'

There's a flickering of eye contact between Carol and her attack dogs, a straightening of the backs of Fashion, Hair and Beauty.

'Frankly, Dr Jones,' says Jenny, the acting head of Fashion amicably. 'We were all anticipating an opportunity to redress the historic gender pay gap within the department.'

And I'm thinking, who's this 'we' she's talking about? Dr Jones turns to her.

'What gender pay gap?!' he asks, looking aghast.

So she tells him.

'Figures I acquired from HR show that the average male earns more than the average female in this department, despite it being dominated by female colleagues.'

There's a well-orchestrated and rehearsed gasp of astonishment from several quarters.

'That's an outrageous accusation,' says Dr Jones. 'Pay grades are devised using benchmark job descriptions and grade profiles in line with other further and higher education institutions and in consultation with trade union representatives. It couldn't be more fair or transparent.'

'That's what they said in Birmingham,' counters Carol in a threatening rasp that turns Dr Jones pale.

He starts tearing strips at the back of his neck again. His mouth begins opening and shutting like a strangled fish, if indeed a fish can be strangled. Carol it seems, has played her psychological joker.

Birmingham City Council's infamous and unfathomable equal pay settlement cost the local tax payer a cool £1 billion in back payments, forcing the local authority to sell off its most profitable and high profile assets and decimating economic regeneration for decades. It also put a stake through the heart of common sense, much like how the discovery of quantum physics dismantled Newtonian physics.

One of the more hideously incomprehensible aspects of quantum physics is that a particle can be in two separate places, and also be two separate things at once. That is, a waveform and a particle. Trying to understand this does your dweedle in, so don't even try. It has flummoxed some of the greatest scientific minds and many are wondering if it can even be understood within the traditional models of science at all. This 'coherent superposition' has been described even by its own exponents as ridiculous, counter intuitive, and turning reality upside down.

What has this got to do with Birmingham and employment law Carl, I hear you ask?

Well, scaling this quantum world up into the 'normal' world would mean a person can be in two jobs at the same time, simultaneously doing completely separate tasks, which is plainly ridiculous. However, we don't need to pump billions into a Large Hadron Collider to study this mystifying phenomenon, we can simply turn to the bizarre world of Birmingham City Council's equal pay settlement to see this 'quantum world' in action.

Two people (let's call them person 'x' and person 'y' so as not to be gender specific) are working for a local 'quantum' council. Person x's 'state' is a dinner lady ('lunchtime server/food advisor') in a warm cafeteria serving meals to school children. Person y's 'state' is a bin man ('refuse collector/loader') heaving putrid bins into the back of a stinking truck in the early hours of a freezing, rain soaked, January morning.

Now, in a 'normal' Newtonian, world, if 'x' wants the pay and bonuses of 'y' then she can get off her fat lazy arse, re-skill and transfer to the other career that pays extra because it is obviously a much more filthy, hazardous and physically demanding job. But in this lunatic 'quantum world' (employment law/public sector) 'x' doesn't need to do that because she IS a bin man already, and can sue the council for not recognising her quantum state and paying her the same as 'y' without having to put in any of the back breaking, dirty work or freezing early morning shifts that 'y' needs to, in order to earn his pay.

In a further incomprehensible twist, she can ALSO

backdate her claim of 'quantum discrimination' for a job she never did for the entire period she never did it, embracing the concept of time travel too. It's like the dinner ladies got Brian Cox and Alan fucking Moore in as barristers.

So successful has this 'quantum discrimination' ('equal value employment') been at making the public sector the efficient, slick operation we see today with its overspend, cutbacks, borrowing and desperate re-capitalisation of the tax coffers, that employment lawyers are now turning their vampiric attention to the private sector in order to make a ubiquitous clusterfuck of the entire fucking economy. It'll be a bit like the Darwin Awards, only at a national economic level. Seriously, the BRIC nations are not exactly shitting themselves at our far sightedness or rushing to emulate our enlightened ways.

Except of course.. Rwanda.

Exactly.

Carol's ominous threat is still hanging in the air and flecks of blood are starting to appear on the raw neck of Dr Jones as he hacks away at it with yellowing nails. It's like witnessing a wounded buffalo being circled by cackling hyenas.

'The department has recruited far more female graduates in recent years who, starting at a lower grade, naturally pull averages down,' protests Dr Jones pathetically.

'The pay gap is not a consequence of men being paid more, it's consequence of the department favouring new female recruits - which is why, as you point out, that there are more females in the department than men!'

He is of course completely missing the point. He's fighting the battle in entirely the wrong arena. This isn't about logic or reality, it's about dethroning the old duffer like the pigs taking over George Orwell's, Animal Farm in the name of Animalism - 'remember always your duty of enmity towards Man and all his ways.' Which in a nutshell is what radical feminism is all about.

Pigs.

Carol grunts.

'You can spin it all you like Dr Jones, the fact remains, there is a gender pay gap and this patriarchal department is discriminating against women.'

His face is now beginning to match the colour of his neck. Blood vessels in his temples that have probably lain dormant for decades are making an appearance.

'It's nothing to do with patriarchy or discrimination,' he says through gritted teeth. 'It's a simple matter of mathematical statistics!'

Like Henry, he needs to learn to just shut the fuck up and look out of the window until his retirement. But he just won't accept that the mentalists have already taken over the asylum. This is the public sector. Contrition and traitorous compliance are the only options open to any normal person. The few men in the room with any testosterone to speak of slink further down into their chairs.

Choose your battles carefully.

Absolutely goddamn right.

Others sit up and pretend to be men-feminists, in a desperate hope they may get laid by the sisters at some unspecified time in the future, like the collaborating, cheese eating, surrender monkeys they are. They'll be the first to have their heads shaved come liberation day.

Carol, sensing the time is ripe for the kill, addresses the room as much as Dr Jones in saying.

'But you are not denying it Dr Jones; you are admitting there IS a gender pay gap?'

Jenny chimes in.

'If a woman was head of department, it would redress the imbalance.'

And that's it.

Under relentless pressure Dr Jones finally raises his head and exposes his jugular.

'Some day, Carol,' he bellows, pointing a shaking finger at her. 'You're just going to have to accept that the person in charge of this department has a penis!'

Far away in the depths of the college, someone drops a pin.

Silence.

'Shizzzzzzz, innit tho?' says the student streaming the entire thing to Youtube from his phone.

Obviously not as disengaged as appearances would first appear. Carol gets to her feet.

'I will not sit here and be harangued by sexist filth.'

And with that she gathers up her notes, picks her way through the huddled mass and out of the library.

'This is blatant institutional misogyny,' echoes Jenny, also standing and accompanying Carol from the library with the other course tutors from Fashion, Hair and Beauty following her like obedient ducklings.

Mary, although initially conflicted, shrugs none the less, and leaves too.

Et tu Brute?

They might be white, metropolitan western feminists, but as the pigs on animal farm believed, 'Man is the only real enemy we have. Remove Man from the scene, and the root cause of hunger and overwork is abolished forever.'

Slowly, one by one, others follow.

The student reps linger slightly longer while they re-tweet the Youtube video, before following suit, delighted at their unprecedented good fortune and only too glad to be leaving a meeting early. Eventually, even the fat, ugly woman from estates gathers up her notes and leaves, worried that the gossip might reach her department before she does.

In the end, only myself, Jeremy, Henry and the sleeping Karen are left. And by the smell of it, her baby has spectacularly shat itself again. Dr Jones, head buried in his hands, bloodied fingertips leaving streaks on his forehead.

It's pretty gross it has to be said.

'Go. The rest of you. Just go,' he whispers through gentle sobs.

Jeremy puts a supportive hand on his shoulder then gestures for Henry and me to leave. We do, in silence, leaving Dr Jones with the rancid smell of deep shit he now finds himself in.

16 RESOURCES

On the cistern, opened at 'Sophie' is a copy of Fiesta that I bought for the Photoshopping module. Try as I might, I haven't been able to punch the clown properly since the psychiatrist put that fucking image in my head of a dog shitting on seafood, and it's driving me to distraction. I'm straddling the disabled toilet on the first floor, one hand leaning hard on the wall, bringing every effort to bear on a petulant cock that refuses to give up it's treasures. A labour of love has become a full on, war of fucking attrition.

Following the mass walk out at the meeting, Dr Jones has announced his early retirement on the grounds of ill health.

She did it.

Carol finally pushed the old cunt over the edge; purged herself of her man-beast in a feminist, version of a Night of the Long Knives.

On the floor, trampled under foot, Men Only.

Since announcing his retirement, Dr Jones is now riding out his notice under self-imposed, house arrest and refuses to leave his office in fear of the college's newly radicalised faminazis. As a result, the department has quickly undergone an ideological annexation. There's been a barrage of emails from Carol, the latest one informing us that the department will, with immediate effect, stop subscribing to magazines or websites that sexualise the female form. Zoo, FHM, Maxim, and Loaded are off the menu for a start because they provide a 'conducive context for violence against women'.

Whatever that means.

She's just returned from a college sponsored skive; a seminar on 'Lose the Lads Mags', with UKfeminista and not only has she got the taste of fresh blood on her lips from the Dr Jones saga, she is also fully re-fuelled on man-hate. The department is to adopt a zero tolerance policy of pornification in the media she tells us via email.

As far as I'm aware, we didn't even subscribe to any 'Lads Mags,' but like any new coup d'état leader, she's issuing diktats early, to keep the masses focused on the ideological agenda while she and her ruling kleptocrats make plans to whore it up in gold enamelled private jets, stroking cats with jewel encrusted fingers and channelling the department's wealth to offshore accounts and state sponsored feminists abroad.

From the pages of Fiesta, Sophie smiles up at me. She doesn't look like the type of woman who would take this type of crap from Carol. As accommodating as Sophie looks, she's not helping me bring forth the baby batter. It's not just waxing the dolphin I'm having problems with, I haven't been able to eat or sleep either. I've lost nearly two kilograms in the past week alone, despite my gym membership running out.

Something has got to give because I can't go on like this.

Dr Jones's demise was swift and brutal even by Carol's standards, and she is now the front runner in a one horse race for Head of Department.

It'll be unbearable.

This is despite the fact that she knows bugger all about any of the industries she is tasked with preparing students for. But education is never about preparing anyone for work as the FSB or CBI will readily attest; it's about setting up students with unrealistic expectations through the medium of unmerited qualifications against a backdrop of a feminized ideology. The last time Carol worked in any industry - graphic design apparently, they were still using letraset and typesetters. She can't even use a computer properly for fuck sake.

On the sink, there's a copy of Vogue - lingerie special, procured from the Fashion department.

The equality act was introduced by feminists and the politically destitute to combat alleged prejudice in the workplace. In reality it just made anti, white-male bias, acceptable and lawful. But like any radical doctrine, feminism is fundamentally a one-trip pony, and once its leaders have achieved their stated goals - in this case, feminizing education and society as a whole, they inevitably turn in on themselves like rats in a barrel. And as society goes to the dogs and the nation slowly slips down world rankings for.. just about everything significant, the revolutionary leaders ditch the values they so fiercely lied about during the pre-revolutionary fervour. In this case, 'equality.' - All animals are equal, but some are more equal than others.

On the towel rail - Bazaar, swimsuit issue, also procured from the Fashion department.

So here's the rub.

When Carol gets the old boy's job, who gets Carol's ?

The favourites are:

- Jenny - Acting head of Fashion
- Karen - Fashion course leader
- Mary – Hair and Beauty course leader

Henry has by far the most years of service, and is still technically in the running but hasn't got a cat in hell's chance on account of the points raised above and him being, well - Henry. So the job comes down to a vociferous black womanist, a sleep deprived, hormonal mother on maternity leave and a radical metropolitan feminist, all apparently determined to bag the job and clambering the hierarchical pyramid of discrimination to actualise their best shot at promotion.

Upper management are literally shitting themselves.

Yes literally.

Whichever way they cut it, it's an inevitable trip to the employment tribunal and they know it. With discrimination against men now backed by legislation, it has inadvertently created a shit storm of complexity. As the dominant silver backs are forced to exit the stage in defeat and humiliation, what follows can only be an object lesson in damage limitation and an abject lesson in crisis management. The impending hostilities will be like trying to referee a Sunday league game between Cosa Nostra and Al fucking Qaeda.

I hit the vinegar stroke over Monica Cruz in a winter 2012 Agent Provocateur ad and I swallow hard as my eyes begin to close, but immediately an image of a dog shitting on seafood comes to mind and the moment's lost.

Again.

On the grab-rail, I-D magazine with Natalia Vodianova modelling Etam's 2014 lingerie line.

Despite being on maternity leave for over two years, the safe money is on Karen. To explain why we'll need to return once more to the unfathomable world of quantum physics.

I know.

I'm sorry.

But bear with me.

Scaling this demented world up into our 'normal' world once again would mean a person can not only be two 'things' at the same time, but simultaneously be in two 'places' at the same time, which again is ludicrous, but employment law comfortably applies this to the real world like so:

Two people (let's call them Henry and Karen so as not to be gender specific) are doing exactly the same job for two years - Head of Course, doing exactly the same hours and achieving exactly the same productivity for their respective courses. Suddenly Karen goes on maternity leave. Two years go by (as it overlaps with getting knocked up a second time), then Karen returns to work. Now in a 'normal' Newtonian world, Henry has four years of on-the-job experience and Karen has only two.

So far so good.

However, in a bizarre 'quantum world', Karen has in fact been in two places at the same time, both on maternity leave, (getting knocked up and having babies) AND at work acquiring exactly the same on-the-job experience as Henry AND getting paid for it. (She has in effect, been paid for having sex, but that's another issue). Therefore, any employer not recognising the quantum state of Karen is in violation of the quantum act, or the equality act as it is more commonly known.

This takes the much vaunted ability of women to 'multi task' to an entirely new level and definitely adds weight to the argument that more women should take up science, because not even Einstein could get his head around the concept, let alone apply it to the real fucking world.

Seriously, the Nobel prize for physics has been awarded for less.

I really can't be worrying about this sort of shit right now, not at this moment in time, not with the position I'm in. So I turn my attention to the job in hand.

I'm beating on this piece of shit more out of spite than pleasure now, trying to break it's fucking spirit. I'm locked in an all-consuming battle of wills; a bitter death struggle with my own cock. I wince at the ache in my wrist but carry on regardless, swallowing again and flipping a page of Fiesta to be confronted by an image of Sophie that would be better placed in a gynaecological textbook. What was the photographer fucking thinking? Seriously, the labia is pulled so far apart, it looks like a squid has been brutally executed between Sophie's legs; like cephalopod homicide - shot through the head with a 9mm pistol. Why anyone would want to shoot a fucking squid in the head is anyone's guess, but frankly it reinforces the need for the continued prohibition on handguns if that's the type of damage they do. Then suddenly there I am again - back to thinking about squids, seafood and that fucking squatting dog again.

I change hands.

Of course in the USA they don't have paid maternity leave at all. Women get a maximum of twelve weeks unpaid leave as long as they meet strict criteria. Some states however grant 'temporary disability' in order for mothers to claim some limited disability insurance. Harsh as this sounds to European ears, it does mean that the economy is in far better shape, productivity is stronger and there are more women in senior and middle management roles than there are in the UK. It probably also goes some way to explain why American kids have a penchant for working through their abandonment issues at school using semi-automatics.

Why they need to use semi automatics when 9mm pistols can do so much damage is anyone's guess.

This is fucking useless.

Squid assassinations and quantum physics aside, I just can't stop thinking about this Carol situation.

On the shelf, Victoria's Secret catalogue - August 2013 edition with Miranda Kerr and Behati Prinsloo, which should be enough to bring anyone to jettison their joy juice.

But no.

I kick the copy of Men Only under the sink, and pull up my sweatpants in defeat. This state of affairs can't go on - I'm too strung out. I gather up the magazines, feeling somewhat aggrieved at the ladies therein for their lamentable inability to spunk my trumpet.

Pornification of the media my arse.

There's no two ways about it, I need to see a professional about the situation, because I can't go on like this.

And I'm thinking.

Where the hell has Casey got to lately?

17 LITERACY, LANGUAGE AND NUMERACY

The radicalization of the college has begun; the purge is underway

The casualties of Carols decree are piling up by the bins at the back of the college. An elephants' graveyard to lost masculinity has been established and a bunch of students are picking their way through the discarded GQ and Esquire magazines from the Fashion department. If it was some growler porn like Hustler or Fiesta I could perhaps understand on the grounds of cephalopod conservation - but seriously, GQ and Esquire?

Fuck sake.

Hustler and Fiesta aside, you can't just ban photos of women like you're the Taliban mafia under the belief it will eradicate something that's hard baked into the DNA of every man.

What the fuck is she thinking?

Evidence of pornographic idolatry goes further back than human civilisation itself. In archaeological circles the 'Venus figurines' found throughout Europe are know as 'religious artefacts' or 'fertility symbols,' but let's be honest, a doll that depicts a passive, faceless woman with 'parts of the body associated with fertility and childbearing highly exaggerated', pretty much nails its colours to the mast of pornography.

When I see Sophie in Fiesta with 'parts of the body associated with fertility and childbearing highly exaggerated' I'm not thinking wow, I really need to attend to my ecumenical responsibilities and reproductive obligations; I'm not thinking dirty nappies, sleepless nights and my whole fucking life clusterfucking into a living nightmare.

No.

I'm not thinking at all.

Papa Smurf is pretty much doing all the thinking for me.

If these 'figurines' weren't designed to get the adolescent Barney and Fred Flintstone tiptoeing to the back of the cave to throw one over the thump, I don't know what was. So why are archaeologists so reluctant to categorise these figurines as ancient porn? They also tell us that these 'mysterious figures,' were generally carried by men during their hunting expeditions away from home as 'lucky charms.'

This tells me three things:

- Archaeologists are dicks and probably feminists
- Objectification of the female form has always been a fundamental part of male sexuality
- We need a national archive to protect today's porn for future historians to marvel over

Mankind has already lost the giant 'Buddas of Bamiyan' to extremist Islamic ideology; it would be a tragedy indeed to also lose 'The Japanese Wife Next Door' to extremist feminist ideology.

Lucky charms my arse.

I pick up a dog-eared copy of Esquire and flick through the pages. There are some hot women but I'm hard pushed to find any tits to justify its place amongst the bins. However, there is an article on the Mercedes SLS AMG black series, and life around me evaporates, as I'm lost in a visceral and covetous desire for the thing. If this bad girl was panting at me from the garage every morning, even the commute to this dump would be worth it. I'm not enjoying or admiring it of course. No. I'm objectifying and exploiting it, and will no doubt go on to abuse or vandalise one whenever I see it, because that's what men's magazines make you do.

Apparently.

I slip it into my bag to read later, no doubt on the bus home.

Pornography, it has to be said, has come a long way since Palaeolithic man carved his first 'Venus figure' and churned his nut mustard all over it. Moreover it has driven evolution and civilisation, and just as those pint sized smoothie makers kick-started a 3D visual art revolution, ushering in the Mesolithic era, modern pornography has accelerated the development of media technologies, from VCRs to streaming video for mobile phones. It is the de facto catalyst for innovation. Demand for pornography has driven the development of core cross-platform technologies for data compression, search engines, micro-payments and file-sharing on which Carol now channels her insidious censorship agenda.

Is that irony or hypocrisy?

Both, it's feminism for fuck sake, and who made these metropolitan radical feminazis the arbiters of morality anyway? Then I hear a voice from the heavens above.

'Can I suggest that if you want to rummage around in bins ogling at filth then you do it in your own time and not in the college's!'

We all look up; me and the students, and see Carol gazing down with pity and scorn, arm outstretched holding open a window like the bastard love child of Benito Mussolini and Harriet Harman.

God I loathe the woman.

Is it any coincidence that Sir Oswald Mosley's, British Union of Fascists became largely driven my women like Carol: Women such as Mary 'Slasher' Richardson and Norah Elam, two of the most preeminent militants of the suffragette movement?

I think not.

In fact the first British Fascist party - The 'Fascisti' was founded in 1923, by the militant feminist, Rotha Beryl Orman.

I blame women's magazines.

They should be banned.

Before I can devise a suitable, wisecracking repost, my phone rings and a number appears on the cracked screen I don't recognise. I've learned from my current financial predicament to field all calls from unknown numbers. When does anyone get good news from an unknown number, ever?

Never. That's when.

Even Camelot doesn't bother to contact you if you win the lottery jackpot, but stay five minutes over your allotted time in a restricted parking bay and the local council put the NSA and GCHQ on the case to track your arse down to the ends of the earth.

Bastards.

When I look up again Carol's gone so I wander back into the building and listen to the message on my phone. It's from Bethany telling me I haven't called Rachel in a week and reminding me of my obligations as a responsible new 'fiancé'.

Shit.

I've got it into my head that this is all just some frikin nightmare that will somehow blow away.

But it won't

I immediately book some seats over the phone for a film I've never heard of in London's South Bank. Here was me thinking it'd be a cheap and cheerful fix but fuck me, the price of cinema tickets has gone up! Then there'll be taxi fares, drinks.. Jesus, we're looking at a hundred notes right there at London prices.

I quickly return Bethany's call and assure her it's all in hand, I just didn't have Rachel's number - an oversight on my behalf, and could she pass on my apologies and the details of my carefully planned date, blah, blah. She seems to buy it, and with that I'm off the hook again until I can figure a way out of this whole debacle.

Then it occurs to me. How can any mother let her daughter out on the streets anyway with all this alleged pornification of the media turning men into chomping-at-the-bit, rapists? Surely they should all be at home hunkering down behind sofa's until Carol and her anti-sexualisation, bingo wing of the feminazis have purged society of this patriarchal menace.

Fuck sake.

Let's do something a bit maverick here; let's go look at some facts instead of lifting the skirt of publicity, jumping onto the stool of self righteous indignation and screaming at the mouse of empirical evidence.

Countries with the most draconian censorship laws have some of the worst sex crime problems. On the other hand, countries with more relaxed attitudes to pornography have relatively low levels of sex crime. Take Japan, a country famed for it's panoply of sexual deviances and a smorgasbord of media platforms on which to deliver them on. It has one of lowest sex crime rates in the civilised world. Contrast that with certain Islam countries and you soon come to realise that pornography, instead of being a threat to the civilised world, is in fact a very effective relief valve which cuts down the amount of perverts using female commuters as humping posts to relieve their sexual frustration.

Am I wrong?

No.

In Afghanistan or the Democratic Republic of Congo for instance, you can't get hold of a copy of 'Loaded' for love nor money, let alone 'Hustler,' but they're hardly feminist utopias now are they? I can't see Carol and her ilk choosing Kinshasa or Kabul over Hebden fucking Bridge for their next spring break, or arranging a SlutWalk down the streets of Islamabad or Riyadh.

Get real.

I look at my phone again, and realise I'd missed another call while sorting out the last missed call. This time it's from the psychotherapist reprimanding me for the missed appointment and telling me I'm at risk of deterioration, relapse and hospital readmission if I don't get in touch ASAP to arrange another one.

As if.

I'm never going near that place again. I've barely been able to eat or sleep since seeing her and buffing the badger has become a grotesque act of animal cruelty, God only knows what other witchcraft the old crow's got hidden up her wizard's sleeve. The NHS doesn't need the Care Quality

Commission; it needs the Witch Finder fucking General.

Walking through reception I catch sight of Jeremy supervising the installation of new display cabinets and I'm half tempted to put him in touch with Svetlana as promised, if only to find out how the scheming cow intends to monetize his expertise. But that would inevitably blow my already shaky Dubai cover story and put an end to any networking prospects. It's like some Scandinavian political drama - but you know, without the shit clothes.

Although on second thoughts, maybe I could do some probing on my own behalf to try and deduce what the fuck she's conniving.

'How goes it Jeremy?' I ask him, in a rare display of joie de vivre.

'Carl!' he squeals in such a high pitched tone that dogs in Shetland start barking.

'I heard you were back at work. How is,' he looks down at my crotch with a pained look, and says 'Everything?'

'Er.. yeah, better thanks. Look if you get a moment, I'd like to just - you know, do a bit of brain-storming over some ideas I've had.'

He waggles a finger sternly.

'You shouldn't be using that phrase Carl; it's, 'thought showering.' he corrects me. 'We don't want to offend people with neurological disorders do we?'

You've got to be kidding me. Thought shower? The workmen elbow each other surreptitiously and give it the rubber wrist at each other.

Dickheads.

'Whatever. Look, I just wanted to maybe discuss ways the college might somehow.. financially benefit by outsourcing it's.. equality and diversity expertise to local firms. Or something.'

He looks at me curiously with a kinda cocked head. Yeah. Now I've said it out loud it sounds even more fucking ridiculous than it sounded in my head. Only a complete fucktard..

'It's like you've been reading my mind,' he whispers, cupping his hands to his mouth. 'I've been writing some proposals on that very idea.'

..would think of something like that.

'Really?'

'Absolutely, maybe we could mail our ideas to each other. Then perhaps - you know, maybe take a thought shower together?'

Oh crap.

'Well it was just a vague idea really,' I tell him, back peddling like crazy. 'Nothing substantial. Send me your stuff though, I'd be interested in.. reading it.'

I head away quickly down the corridor.

Fuck me, that was close.

18 INFORMATION AND COMMUNICATION TECHNOLOGY

I'm reading an email:

Subject: Notice of disciplinary hearing.

Dear Mr Waxman

I am writing to inform you that you are required to attend a disciplinary hearing on Monday 3rd February at 9am which is to be held in the college's main board room.

At this meeting the question of disciplinary action against you, in accordance with the College Disciplinary Procedure, will be considered with regard to:

- Wilful refusal to comply with reasonable management instruction
- Deliberately falsifying stakeholder records
- Using grossly offensive behaviour towards a colleague

- Incapacity at work through an excess of drugs
- Using college equipment to access pornographic material during work time
- Inappropriate relations with stakeholders

Due to the serious nature of these claims, the possible consequences arising from this meeting might be:

- Immediate Dismissal for Gross Misconduct in line with College's Disciplinary Procedure.

You are entitled, if you wish, to be accompanied by a work colleague or a trade union representative.

Yours sincerely

Mr John Davies - Deputy Dean

*

So it's me; I'm next on Carol's hit list.

This job is the only thing that facilitates the drip, drip feed that services my loans and holds off the debt collection agencies and as shit as it is; I'd be buggered without it. It's the only thing preventing the repossession of my apartment.

I send the email to the printer to start making notes on it. Of course when I go to collect the printout the printer has a problem: Error 3508, it tells me.

What am I, R2 fucking D2?

I ring up tech support and read out the number from the printer display window. They tell me it's out of ink and to fill in a form to replace the ink cartridge.

Fill in a form?

Being the pro-active type I ignore this advice and remove the cartridge from the machine and take it to the tech support room myself for a replacement. Standing in front of the desk of a greasy haired twelve year old, waiting for him to acknowledge my presence I feel like the butler to little Lord Fauntleroy. I cough and finally he looks up at the ink cartridge in my hand, horrified at my resourcefulness.

'Oh, no, you're not supposed to take it out,' he informs me, wide eyed. 'You have to fill in a PRHP03 and WE replace it.'

'Well I've saved you a job; I've got it right here,' I tell him, holding the cartridge out to him. 'Just give me a replacement and I'll do it myself.'

He backs off and refuses to take it. Even though every job advert I've ever seen claims to be looking for people with initiative, in the public sector it just breeds panic and confusion. He shakes his head.

'It's not - you know, policy,' he tells me.

I look at the stack of printer cartridges behind his desk and back at him. This is going nowhere.

'Fine,' I tell him. 'Give me one of your forms and I'll fill it in.'

'You have to download it from the college intranet,' he says turning back to his screen. 'You have to print it out, fill it in, then put it in the tray over there. It then gets sorted on order of priority,' he informs me, like I'm some goof.

He flicks his head to a pile of papers in the corner of the room that looks like it hasn't been touched in days. Is he taking the piss? I've been here before with these forms. I might as well make a paper aeroplane with it and fly it out of the bloody window.

'Let me get this straight. You're telling me to print a form from a printer that doesn't work to tell you it isn't working?'

He sighs, and gives me a withering, look.

'There are other printers in the college dude.'

Dude now is it? I'll 'dude' the little shit if he doesn't give me a fucking replacement cartridge soon.

'My credit account doesn't work in other departments,' I inform him politely.

'Library?' He offers.

'It's, ' I lower my voice, not quite believing I'm about to say this. 'It's 25p a sheet in the library, I'm not paying those prices!'

He sits back and sucks his teeth.

'Woh, that's gone up!' he observes.

Yes it has you little dweeb; now give me a fucking cartridge.

'Hey, I know!' I tell him, like I've just had some goddamn life changing epiphany and pointing to the printer in the corner of the room. 'How about you just print me one out here?'

He glances at this colleague sat at the opposite desk, possibly his superior who also looks like a twelve year old, but with a sort of beard thing and wearing Crocs over odd socks. I guess he thinks he's being kinda eccentric or something but it just makes him look even more of a cock than he already is.

'No can do, amigo,' he says, coming to the defence of Little Lord Fauntleroy.

Amigo now?

'That comes out of OUR budget see?'

Clearly my dispute has now been escalated up the chain of command to the odd-sock-and-Croc freak. I look at the cartridge in my hand and again at the pile of boxed cartridges behind Little Lord Fauntleroy. I look at the untouched pile of forms then have a thought.

'What gets highest priority?' I ask the Croc freak.

He looks at me suspiciously.

'Error 387 obviously'

Obviously. Little shit.

'And what is that in English?'

'The printer needs replacing. The rental company brings a replacement and takes the faulty one back. Same day service.'

*

Back at the office, everyone is either throwing a sicky or teaching.. mostly throwing a sicky, so I've got the cover off the printer and in the process of striking down upon it with great vengeance and furious anger with a large screw driver I borrowed off the caretaker or, 'site engineer' when Jeremy walks in.

'What are you doing?' he asks, with genuine curiosity.

'Erm.. fixing the printer,' I tell him unconvincingly.

He points at the display.

'Oh. you've got an Error 387,' he informs me.

'You'll never fix that. I had one a few months ago. You need to call tech support and they'll replace it immediately.'

Bingo.

'Really? Thanks, I'll try that.'

With my goal achieved and my face speckled with printing ink blood, I stand up with a sigh of deep satisfaction.

'What can I do for you?' I ask him.

'It's more of a question of what I can do for you,' he tells me. 'I was wondering if you've had time to look through those equality and diversity initiatives I emailed to you, but..'

He shakes his head and sighs.

'Then I heard about this disciplinary hearing thing and wondered if you needed anyone to represent you?'

For a glorious moment there, while mutilating the printer, it had completely escaped my mind. Blood lust can be very cathartic and absorbing sometimes.

'I hadn't given it much thought,' I admit.

He puts his hand gently to his chest.

'Please Carl, I know you've got a lot on your mind at the moment so I would consider it an honour and a privilege if you would let me represent you and prepare your defence. I have a great deal of experience with college policy and procedure, and besides,' he says, leaning in close like he's letting me in on a little secret. 'I'm in the process of completing my MOOC in equality law.'

Nope; no idea what that is. No fucking clue. I shrug. I guess if the chutney ferret wants to put some extra time in on my behalf, it can't do any harm.

'Ok Jeremy, erm.. thanks.'

'No, thank YOU Carl. It'll be a great opportunity for me to try out some of my new skills. Oh dear, look you've got some ink on your lovely Ted Baker shirt.'

I look down at the flecks of black ink on my shirt

'Shit. It's the only decent Ted Baker I have left.'

He steps forward and licks a monogrammed handkerchief taken from his Paul Smith shirt.

'Here let me just..'

He presses it firmly to my chest, blotting the stain. My back is against the printer so I can't move. It's.. unnerving.

'I just want to say what an inspiration you are Carl,' he says, pinning me to the printer with his finger.

'You're always punctual, immaculately presented and in meetings you're so.. reserved and dignified. I admire your silent resolve, your fair non-judgmental manner and above all, the way you don't just talk about equality and diversity, you APPLY it.'

He breathes me in.

'You really are an inspiration.'

Get me, an inspiration.

'In my opinion, this disciplinary hearing is a pernicious conspiracy by a few envious individuals and I will not stand by and see you bullied like this,' he says, almost angrily.

'Erm.. thanks Jeremy,' I tell him again, still pinned to the printer.

'You know,' he says looking directly into my eyes.

'What we need right now.. is to introduce a little alcohol or perhaps amyl nitrate into the situation.'

Oh, crap.

'Oh yeah.. erm.. but you know what.. I don't think you're allowed those sort of things at work?' I tell him, panicked by his sudden chutzpah.

'To get things moving,' he says, making a little circular motion with his finger.

'Er yeah.. pretty sure that's a no. Not during working hours any-hoo,' I laugh nervously.

'For the stain, silly. It neutralises the pigment in the ink!'

He laughs too. We both laugh. I breath out. Thank fuck. Here was me thinking..

'Why, are you suggesting we could maybe think about it AFTER work sometime?'

Oh shit, oh shit, oh shhhitt.

'I er.. well..'

Mercifully, from nowhere, Mary comes crashing into the office. Seeing us at the printer, she comes to a juddering halt, before awkwardly folding her immense arse under the table like a deflating bouncy castle. Jeremy suddenly backs off and stares at her.

'Mary?!'

Mary puts a finger to her lips.

'!' she hisses at him.

Jeremy puts his hand to his mouth again in horror, and turns to me with an expression of regret and panic.

'Oh my god!' he says, looking quickly around the room

before deciding there's no-where to hide and making a sharp exit out of the door.

It must be that time of year again.

When a Roman commander returned victorious from a foreign campaign, he was afforded the privilege of a civil ceremony known as a Triumphal Procession. In this procession the captives of the vanquished army, were made to walk through the city in front of victorious commander in humiliation. Limping and wounded, these captive tribesmen and their families; these strange, exotic people from far away lands were paraded before the free citizenry of Rome, to satisfy their curiosity and to glorify the conquering hero.

Carol is on the move.

As Deputy Head (soon to be Head) of the Faculty of Art, Design and Media, the task of coordinating the prospectus photo shoot falls to her, and she takes to the role with vigour. She has dredged departments and corridors of all oddities, minorities and disabilities; all creeds and colours, the mentally and physically challenged and infirm, to form a triumphal procession to glorify her equality and diversity credentials. She wheels the vacant wheelchair before her like a chariot, kept in a storeroom alongside the scull caps, turbans, crutches, saris and jubbahs for just such occasions, driving the procession on; whipping it with her tongue.

'Move along everyone, I've only got the equipment signed out for a few hours. Go, go, go!'

She stops at the office door and seeing me stood there asks.

'Have you seen Mary, we seem to have lost her?'

The royal 'we' I notice.

'I need her for the next shoot.'

I look up and to my right, doing 'remembering'. From the corner of my eye I see Mary putting her hands together in prayer doing 'pleading'. I'm harbouring a fugitive. How did it come to this?

'What does she look like?' I ask, stalling for time.

There's only one way to describe Mary, and that's 'big and black,' but as Carol tells anyone who is forced to listen, she would never 'define or 'categorise' a person by 'colour,' 'physique' or 'disability.' Unless of course she's doing a prospectus . Then she 'defines' and 'categorises' with all the zeal of a Nazi commander clearing a sectarian ghetto.

'You know.. she's.. a person of colour? From Hair and Beauty,' she tells me.

I do 'remembering' again.

'What colour?' I ask.

Carol looks at me with undisguised contempt.

'I take it you've read your emails this morning?' she says, curtly changing the subject and turning the corners of her mouth up in a kinda snarl/smile combo.

Seeing the look on my face she tells me.

'I warned you Carl. You've only got yourself to blame.'

Bitch.

'See you at the hearing,' she says, waving her fingers at me. 'Ta ta.'

And with that, she's gone, driving on her captive horde - her multi-national humanitarian crisis. The same faces and wheel chair displaced from department to department, appearing on every page, on every course of the college prospectus.

These poor innocents, singled out for their disabilities, ethnicities, body shapes and colour; paraded before the cameras and shot. It's false and deceptive representation; it's spreading false, propaganda like Leni Riefenstahl casting 'Triumph of the Will' or worse, a BBC director casting.. anything really.

I should report it.

But I won't.

Whistle blowers are rarely given a comfortable ride over this sort of thing, and so instead I watch in horrid guilty fascination, afraid to speak out.

I am no Edward Snowden.

I am no Bradley Manning.

I am the ordinary bystander who obeys the laws while victimisation goes on all around, just trying to avoid the terrorising activities of an oppressive regime, fearful of the reprisals if I show any sign of disapproval. Instead I remain passive and indifferent until some opportunity presents itself to make a small defiant act. Hiding Mary is my token subversion against tyranny - the Anne Frank in my attic, so to speak. Although with the best will in the world I'd never get Mary into an attic without the aid of heavy lifting equipment.. which would kinda give the game away.

When the danger has passed, Mary slowly unfolds herself from under the table and leans against the wall with a look of relief.

'Tank-you, honee,' she says. 'You save my life. Every year with this stupid, stupid photo-shoot ting.'

She shakes her head and comes ambling over and takes me up in a great bear hug that completely engulfs me. It leaves me with a warm glow to see her expression. This is what Joseph Schindler must have felt like.

She checks the coast is clear but turns around in the doorway, looking a little confused.

'You know honee?' she informs me with a slight smile.

'I never took you for a batty boy.'

'Huh? No! Me and Jeremy? It was just.. we were..'

'Iss cool honee,' she says reassuringly. 'We're all part of God's glorious plan.'

Then she exits the room, heading down the corridor in the opposite direction from Carol.

Jesus, I need to nip that rumour in the bud before it takes off on the college grapevine. I contemplate running after her to put her straight, but I'm fretting about the stain on my Ted Baker shirt too much. Instead I quickly return the screwdriver to the caretaker and ask him urgently to point me in the direction of some amyl nitrate or rubbing alcohol.

Which he does.

With a wink.

Fucknut.

19 RECORD KEEPING

I haven't been on a bike in over twenty years.

What the hell was I thinking?

If I'd known that one day I'd be in a job that would necessitate commuting on a fucking town bike, I'd have wrapped my maw around the exhaust pipe of my BMW - you know, before it was repo'd.

But I didn't.

This regrettable state of affairs was forced upon me following my nauseating foray onto public transport. I should have learned by now, anything with a 'public' prefix can only mean inefficiency, squalor, shame, filth and expense; public sector, public opinion, public health, public funding, public swimming pool, public humiliation and public execution! That cursed word merely draws down eternal damnation on anything it affronts.

Naively, on buses, I thought maybe everyone just gets to

stare out of the window and mind their own business. Occasionally you might get the odd drunk trying to talk to you if you're unlucky, but after ignoring him long enough he generally moves on to the Granny in the disabled seating at which point you can breathe a sigh of relief, content in the knowledge that you've delayed her discomfort somewhat by acting as a decoy, like the have-a-go hero you are.

But always there are babies crying and kids singing the wheels on the bus go round and round and round and round, while their morbidly obese mother ignores the annoying little fuckers because she's too busy texting her mate about the slapping Gary gave to her because she'd shagged some other cunt the week before, who's progeny she'll eventually end up burdening the tax payer with along with the rest of her brood like the parasitic, bingo winged, slapper she is. Gary on the other hand will be shacked up with some other tart by this time and starting another freeloading brood like the metastasised cancer cell on society he is too.

There's always, some testosterone fuelled duchebag, with his feet on the seats, looking like he's been dipped in sticky toffee pudding and wearing a t-shirt, hanging open like its been savaged by an angry rodent after a particularly gruelling session of gerbelling. He usually has a baseball cap and tattoos that look like they've been traced from a magazine using a bic and poster paint. This preening erection with his stupid haircut; this depressing echo of a lost British masculinity has his arms slung over some orange, bejewelled Julie, chewing her gum and chain snapping selfies like the narcissistic pikey she is.

Foreign students on the top deck looking frightened and bemused, surrounded by hoodies who are draped over seats, off their faces on solvent and communicating in some form of unintelligible patois. You can tell they're foreign students because they're dressed in tasteful clothes, speak in full sentences and aren't gobbing or swearing at anyone; something that will always mark you out as a foreigner. These foreign students are always huddled together wondering what kind of planet they've landed on. This wasn't the fucking country they signed up to! In the college prospectus, Britain was a Danny Boyle-esce, multicultural and homosexual utopia with no scary white/orange people, where everyone is mentally retarded but happy with their special needs and overly friendly, and all whizzing around in wheelchairs singing One fucking Direction songs.. way out of key obviously, because they're all deaf too.

After just one week exposed to this Ken Loach scripted nightmare, I realised I needed to make other arrangements.

Following a misguided bid on Ebay I 'won' myself a town bike. Following my initial elation at acquiring the thing, I'm now in the midsts of a reality check.

This is the type of situation that creeps up on you when you aren't paying close attention to the shit direction your life plan is headed; like the proverbial boiling frog. Now I'm staring at the sides of the pan wondering how the hell I got in here, and why would anyone want to boil a frog anyway? That sort of cruelty doesn't make any fucking sense whatsoever and never will, and not for the first time, I'm forced to ponder the fact that kids are all evil little shits.

For a brief moment back then, when I was bidding, I had visions of being the wingman to Bradley Wiggins or better still, Lance Armstrong, hurtling along the road on a drug fuelled high, getting fit, looking buff, drawing adulation and winning medals. Five minutes in commuter traffic brought that hazy, delusional crap into sharp focus. I've never won any medals for anything in my life and for some reason that still doesn't seem fair. But then that's the type of unrealistic expectation that an equality obsessed society and watching the fucking Olympics puts in your head. Nobody draws adulation or wins medals for anything in the real world and the sooner we all realise that the easier it'll be on everyone. But it still seems fucking unfair. Maybe I should talk to Jeremy or the college's pastoral support officer about it.

I've been slapped by wing mirrors and run off the road by women texting, twittering, applying make-up or making a three course dinner in their shitty little Kia Picantos. I've been screamed at by fat, bald men in white vans and had half eaten kebabs thrown at me by obese kids who have no appreciation of food waste, the fat little fucks. Don't they know there's Africans starving all over the world?

I've quickly come to realise that commuting by bike will have me dead within the week.

Catching my reflection in the windows of McDonalds does nothing for my self esteem either. I look neither fit nor buff in my fluorescent lycra and piss pot helmet. I couldn't afford a decent racer so ended up with a sort of sit up and beg type bike that makes you look like a girl, or a middle aged Dad in the midst of a mid life crisis who claims to be saving the planet for his kids to trash at some unspecified time in the future.

Bollocks, you just can't afford a Porsche you sad cunt.

I negotiate the roundabouts and take the abuse because it's either this or public transport. When I was on the bus I wiped away the condensation and looked out in envy at the freedom of the cyclists; now I'm on the bike I'm wishing I was back on the bus. As cold sleet begins to spatter my face, mingling with warm tears of regret, I realise that all I really, really want is the soft, leathery cocoon of my gorgeous BMW - something that will never happen ever again as long as I remain in this godforsaken job, because the only people who can afford top end BMW's in the public sector are dinner ladies in fucking Birmingham.

It's 9:30am by the time I reach college so the place is still virtually deserted and I'm spared the humiliation of walking a gauntlet of stares, taunts and questions about my beloved car. I lock the bike to the railings, take off my helmet and hurry into the building. My ball is aching from the commute and is just another unforeseen level of pain and humiliation that makes the whole situation even more harrowing and wrong than it already is. I give the lonely fella a gentle massage and reminisce on our happier times together.

I slip the rucksack from my shoulder containing my work clothes, and head for the disabled toilets relieved I've made it into work alive and relishing the prospect of peeling off this wet lycra and soggy bandage around my groin. I plan to spend at least half an hour squatting under the hand dryer to warm up and dry off before facing the rest of the day. When your only place of respite and comfort is a disabled toilet, it's very, very easy to begin losing faith in yourself.

I try the door of the toilet but for some reason it's locked. Which is weird. This has never happened before. The caretaker must have deadlocked it; finally cottoning on to the fact that no one with any physical disability to speak of could possibly reach it anyway with the lift the way it is. I rattle the handle a few times just to make sure, like that ever made a difference to any lock. It doesn't, and in a final act of ironic sabotage to my dignity, I realise even the disabled toilets have been closed to me.

'Just a moment!' says a voice, before another one quickly cuts it off with a, 'shhh!'

Who in Gods name?! I can't believe some shameless cunt is using the disabled toilet as a shag room.. at this time in the morning. No one in this godforsaken place would possibly have that much imagination or resourcefulness, unless.. oh God, unless it's Casey. Surely she wouldn't? I don't think my ego could take another knock this morning.

I feel horribly betrayed. Casey, you are dead to me.

The bolt slides back and slowly the unmistakable face paint of Hilary from Hair and Beauty, peers from behind the door.

The dirty slut!

'I'll just be a minute,' she tells me gingerly.

I put my hands on my hips, in an exaggerated display of vexation, but stood in multi-coloured lycra as I am, it probably just looks really fucking camp.

'Is there someone else in there with you?' I ask indignantly, tapping my foot, but secretly relieved Casey, in my own mind at least, remains faithful.

Hilary looks hesitantly back into the room, pauses for an unnecessarily long time, then back at me.

'Erm.. no,' she tells me, hooking some ruffled hair behind her ear.

In the mirror behind her I see a figure cowering in the corner. He's got boxer shorts around his ankles and his shirt hanging open with the lights from the ceiling reflecting off his large, white albino torso.

And he's got the biggest cock I have ever seen on a man or beast.

'Jesus Christ! Are you and Henry... fucking in there?'

There are many, many laws within the observable universe, some of which we are yet to understand, but Henry fucking Hilary in the disabled toilets with a colossal schniedelwutz, doesn't feature in any one of them.

'We're just fulfilling our physical needs.. like normal healthy people!' protests Hilary.

Ah, Jesus stop. Normal? Normal! I want to peal my flesh off with a sharp crucifix then baste myself with caustic soda. Not even in some parallel multiverse would this feature as 'normal'. It's a defilement that goes beyond a reality already so thoroughly defiled that the bravest of men can do nothing but weep in the streets at the filth, shame depravity and sheer evilness of it all.

'Why?!' I shout at the gap.

Which makes no sense at all. I am not interested why they're fucking in the disabled toilet or why Henry has a titanic truncheon. It's like asking why God allows evil things to happen in the world. There's no logical reason. Why did I even ask that? Don't answer that Hilary, for fuck sake, I just don't have the perceptual sagacity to process such theological conundrums.

'Please don't tell anyone Carl!' pleads Henry from the back of the room, like some bleating teenager.

Somehow this just makes it worse. I could have walked away, pretended not to notice, but now.. now my name has been brought into the situation I'm forever part of the sexual narrative that is Hilary and Henry. I'm being dragged in, deeper and deeper. I need to tear off my clammy wet clothes and burn them, then throw myself onto the pyre too. I'm hoping maybe I can die at any moment and this episode in my life will be forgotten and lost in the midsts of time.

But I don't.

And it's not.

And it's yet another reason I should have wrapped my maw around the exhaust pipe of my BMW when I had the fucking chance, because the image of Henry stood behind Hilary; stood there with his MONSTER COCK..

..is probably going to stay with me for the rest of my goddamn life.

20 TEACHING AND LEARNING APPROACHES

It's Saturday afternoon. What I'm wearing, is a burlesque, steel boned brocade little number with matching panties in a delicate red lace trim. Where I am, is the penthouse roof terrace of Miles's weekend retreat in Brighton. Party time is never far away with Miles and with his finger ever on the pulse of the festivity zeitgeist, he has invited a select gathering to his SlutWalk-inspired shebang, to coincide with Brighton's annual SlutWalk. Luckily he seems blissfully unaware of my little escapade with the Weiners and if he does know, he hasn't let on. Surprisingly Svetlana has turned up too - without Bartek.

A SlutWalk party is much like a Rocky Horror party with less emphasis on the Rocky and more on the Horror. Below the balcony, far, far below, a bunch of fur lappers amble past in various modes of undress, waving banners, protesting at, or showing support for a range of pressing issues such as:

- Pro-intersectionality
- Anti-kyriarchy
  And without a hint of irony
- Lose the Lads Mags

I'm no fan of focus groups as a basis for co-ordinating a marketing strategy, but perhaps on this occasion it wouldn't have been a bad idea. I raise a glass in salute.

'Go sisters!'

Svetlana, looking very doable in a taffeta, over-busted lingerie number in burgundy and black comes over and tops my glass up from the bottle of Dom Perignon 2003 she's procured from the champagne bin. Like most of the party-goers, we're both off our tits on the Columbian dust thoughtfully provided by Miles. Earlier we were playing the SlutWalk version of 'Who am I,' where we tried to guess which psycho-bitch was written on our foreheads. It was hilarious for all of thirty seconds, until someone realised they'd used a permanent marker and the writing had transferred through the postit notes and tattooed our fucking foreheads. Svetlana tries in vane to rub Alanis Morrisette off my forehead by gobbing on it and wiping it with a serviette, with very limited success.

Why do psycho bitches all have such long fucking names?

'How is balls and vinky now?' she asks, barely able to conceal a smile as she looks down at the bulge in my panties.

'Fine,' I inform her, not wanting to linger on such a sore point.

It's not fine, the bulge is due to about half a metre of sterilised gauze wrapped around my bollocks which the skimpy panties are ill designed to conceal.

Miles ambles over in a sheer black mosh playsuit, which has obviously been tailored to fit the larger figure and barely concealing his raging horn for Svetlana. He hooks an arm over both of our shoulders, briefly glancing at Svetlana's tits before directing his attention at the parade below.

'Fuck me, someone call Sea Shepherd!'

Svetlana follows his gaze and stares and stares at the parade bumping and grinding it's way down Grand Parade like some body dysmorphic zombie-walk. The expression on her face is a picture of complete incomprehension.

'Vot ugly prostitutes protest about?' she asks, watching the parade in horrid fascination.

Where to start.

'They want equality and - you know, that sort of thing.' Is about all I can be arsed with by way of explanation.

'They want same equality-diversity as beautiful prostitutes?!' she asks, still grappling with the whole concept.

I shrug.

'That's feminism for you,' I tell her sagely, making no sense whatsoever.

Then Miles in a total about turn like the hypocrite he is, starts pointing.

'I'd do her... and her.'

They say a man thinks about sex about once every seven seconds. Which of course, is bollocks. If you ever see the footage of a combat drone; those grainy black and white images with crosshairs constantly jumping second by second between potential targets, flown by a pilot far, far away - that's a man's brain. Sex works on a kind of 24-hour autopilot deep in the subconscious. Like a woman has an extra stomach for chocolate, a man has a separate consciousness for sex. It's why men are so much better at things like maths, science and IT. Men are constantly checking, reviewing and analysing potential targets and data, even when you think they're not. EVEN when you see someone like - say, Steven Hawkins lecturing in some intellectual depth on the subject of black hole event horizons, his man brain is flicking about the audience picking out potential targets - do her.. do her.. do her. It's why he has that odd grin on his face all the time and why he wants more women to take up science.

'And her... , maybe her,' Miles continues.

Svetlana looks at him in disgust.

'You no need to fack with ugly English prostitutes! I get you best beautiful prostitutes from Ukraine!'

One of the reasons Western feminism is failing to engage women like Svetlana from other parts of the world, is because it attempts to take a great big ideological dump on cultural values and principles instead of engaging with the foreign sisters and their traditions at a local level. Take the Czech Republic and Slovakia as an example.

It's traditional for girls and women to be beaten with a ceremonial stick called a 'pomlazka' during the Easter festival, in the hope that this will keep them as supple as the willow branches they are beaten with. It apparently keeps them young, healthy, beautiful and fertile. It's like beauty therapy and IVF all thrown into one. And in accordance with tradition, the girls are so pleased with this 'beating' that they shower the men who beat them with gifts.

It's win-win when you think about it.

Miles, tears his eyes from the psycho parade below and refocuses again on Svetlana's tits.

'Really? We should talk business, because I know a lot of people who would pay top dollar for Eastern European women. You're all so damned.. sexy.'

Fuck sake.

Only Miles would use the ruse of a prostitution racket as a pick-up line.

It's only a thought, but perhaps if SlutWalk organisers dovetailed practices such as 'pomlazka' beatings into their demonstrations in the interests of multiculturalism, the likes of Svetlana and her Eastern European sisters might better engage with the ideology of Western feminism. And just thinking outside the box again for a second, Latino and Hispanic sisters could be brought on board too with a 'Running With The Bulls' type scenario. Chasing half dressed women through the streets with large sticks may also interest extreme Islamic advocates too, perhaps offering an opportunity for an olive branch between the two fundamentalist cultures.

I don't want to suggest completely losing the spirit of SlutWalks and neither am I completely blind to the perceived 'mixed message' this might engender, but with a bit of give and take, it could offer an opportunity to bring the two fundamentalist cultures together; an opportunity for the sisters and the Muslim brotherhood to find some common ground perhaps.

It's a fine balancing act I know, and you walk a tight rope of diplomacy with these sort of things, but it's the type of Third Way political thinking that got us through the Northern Island troubles and apartheid in South Africa. Throw in some foam machines and dry ice and you could put the 'fun' back into fundamentalism. I'll wager I wouldn't be the only man willing to participate in such an event and be proud to, temporarily at least, call myself a man feminist.

Honestly, if that doesn't win the 'Distinguished Feminist Award' for outstanding contributions to feminist culture, then it's proof, if proof were needed that feminists are just hypocritical, sexist scum.

Jesus, I really need to lay off the powder.

'More champagne?' I ask Miles and Svetlana, being the gentleman that I am. Svetlana, chugs what's left in her glass and tells me.

'Get bottle from bin. When you come back I vont to talk more about equality-diversity. You still have not given number to me of your Jeremy!' she scolds.

I *facepalm* and tell her.

'I forgot. But stay right here because I really want to

discuss that with you.'

I exit quickly, leaving her talking to Miles about the logistics of bumping fuzz with one of her Ukrainian prostitutes.

Being Brighton, Caroline Lucas, the Green MP is there shaking her tushie in support of the feminism.. and the environment, and local TV is showing the SlutWalk live. Some rookie reporter is running along side one of the Sluts and breathlessly asking.

'Isn't this march just an example of women defining their sexuality on male terms?!'

The grizzly munter in a bra sack at least two sizes too small for her, shouts back.

'We are tired of being oppressed by slut-shaming; of being judged by our sexuality and feeling unsafe!'

And you only have to look at her once to be thinking.

You wish.

The camera quickly cuts to a scuffle where a group of Muslim men dressed in traditional Islamic jubbahs and skull caps are trying to throw 'modesty blankets' over the SlutWalkers and failing miserably. It's like watching fisherman trying to catch humpback whales with handkerchiefs, but if they can wrestle just one of those Cetaceans into a burka, then it has to be well worth the struggle.

At the toilet I take a long awaited piss then redress my balls with some fresh gauze I had the foresight to bring along, before returning to the party. I pick up another bottle of

Dom and peel off the foil as I pass the TV and the tart is still banging on.

'Being in charge of our sexual lives should not mean that we are opening ourselves to an expectation of violence!'

It's riveting. And with that, she's swept up in a heaving mass of sweaty blubber.

Idly, I unwrap the wire from the bottle as I await the next thrilling instalment. Next, the reporter turns to a group following up the rear and I damn near drop the bottle. It's Maria, Chantelle-Jo and Casey heading up a group of other students from the college in cheap lingerie.. and Hijabs - stained with fake blood. Chantelle-Jo is waving a placard that reads simply:

'Hijab SLUTS!'

Casey is blissfully unaware that her 'Hijab' is actually a blue and white Jewish headscarf with a star of David on it. Above it she's waving a banner saying.

'Stop shooting Muslim Girls!'

?!

'This is a bit political!' says the reporter nervously looking further down the parade route where the counter demonstration of Muslim men is making its presence felt.

'What message are you sending out here?'

Good question.

Chantelle-Jo steps forward, and grabbing the mike shouts.

'Thanks!'

Like she's just won x-factor or something, then just stairs into the camera like a rabbit caught in headlights. The reporter tries to wrestle the microphone back without success, then gives up and just lowers her face to it and yells

'Er.. who exactly are the Hijab SLUTS?!'

Chantelle-Jo, oblivious to the cacophony around her, a fixed grin looking straight to camera and looking suddenly very self conscious and lost for words blurts out.

'It's a college project really. It was our tutor's idea.'

'No it fucking wasn't!' I shout at the TV impotently.

Then behind her the rest of the girls start whooping, squealing and jumping about like meerkats on a hot plate, but - you know, wearing lingerie and headscarfs and holding placards. No forget it. The drugs are messing with my similes. It's a televised clusterfuck of insults aimed at the most volatile people on the planet, and there she is telling the entire world, it's my idea. At least she hasn't mentioned me by name.

'Hi Carl!' shouts Casey waving at the camera.

She kisses the lens then draws a heart in the lipstick smear left behind. Then they all join in, with cheerful whooping like they're partying in fucking Ibiza.

I'm toast.

Bumping my way through the party crowd, I head back to

the roof terrace. I hang over the rails and scan the sea of flesh, taffeta and oestrogen abhorrence to locate the TV camera and the 'Hijab Sluts.' Staring slack jawed, I suddenly feel sick. The TV reporter has now been joined by photographers and others hacks, keen to get photos and more insightful sound bites from the girls. From the TV, I hear Chantelle-Jo has now found her voice again, saying.

'Yeah like, we support Masala and hate the Muslims and Koreans what shot her. Go Masala girl! Whooooo!'

More whooping and cheering.

'I need to go,' I tell Miles and Svetlana, turning for the door. 'I need to shut those idiots up.'

I don't even wait for the lift. I take the stairs four at a time, doing untold damage to my groin that the drugs and Krug completely prevent me from registering. The counter demonstration of Muslim men has moved and is now blocking the door of Miles's apartment block. Pushing my way through the sea of jubbahs and taqiyah skull caps I notice I still have the bottle of champagne in my hand, but I'm loathed to leave it on the street for some Brighton skank to demolish it, so I use it as a battering ram to get through the crowd. I'm jostled violently and suddenly propelled into the heart of the parade itself, just as the Hijab Sluts banners bare down on me. I shout at the girls and mercifully on seeing me, they turn their attention from the reporters and with more whooping and shouting descend on me.

'Carl!' shouts Casey, throwing her arms around me and turning back to the reporters, telling them. 'This is Carl! This is our tutor, right over here!'

The hacks and photographers surge forward. One guy shoves a huge lens right in my face and starts snapping away.

'Fuck me mate!' he says between the clicks and whirs. 'Have you got a death wish or something?!'

I push the lens away and waving the bottle of champagne at the girls shout to them.

'Hey, you wanna maybe get out of here and.. come to a party or something?'

I thumb the doorway behind me and more whooping follows. When did this stupid fucking 'whooping' thing begin? I manage to get Casey, Chantelle-Jo and Maria to follow - unfortunately bringing their media throng along with them. But the route back to the pavement has now well and truly been blocked by the counter demonstration of the Muslim men.

'Where are the fucking police?!' shouts one of the Sluts, pleading protection from a man in authority.

Naturally.

Pushed up against the hairy beard of a Muslim or feminist, it's hard to tell which, I see in their mirrored shades something scrawled above my right eye in smudged black, permanent marker:

Alah!

Holy Fuck.

The beard lunges at me with such a guttural shout I think I actually piss my panties. Either that or the gauze has unravelled and blood is now running down my bare leg.

Next up there's a loud pop, and some idiot shouts, 'Gun.' and there's pandemonium as people run around in panic going precisely nowhere. The cork from my champagne bottle makes a smooth ark over the heads of the crowd hitting an approaching police helmet. A fountain of champagne follows it into the air covering the devout Muslims in Dom Perignon's finest, which turns the pandemonium into a full blown fucking riot.

21 COMMUNICATION, BEHAVIOUR AND RESPECT

Another day, another memo with yet more linguistic periphrases. It's not, 'special needs' anymore it's, 'additional needs.' It's not, 'mixed race' anymore it's, 'mixed heritage.' It's not 'ethnic minority' anymore it's, 'minority ethnic.' Seriously, 'minority ethnic,' what's the difference? I put my head in my hands. I don't know how much more of this shit I can take.

Still battered and bruised from the SlutWalk I'm sat in the disabled toilet with my head in my hands. I probably would have sat there all day if it weren't for the call over the PA from Dr Jones's secretary informing me there were 'gentlemen' in his office to see me.

And so it begins.

The footage of the 'SlutWalk Riot' and the 'Hijab SLUTS' has been trending - particular in the Middle East. 'Muslims Drenched In Champagne' has had over 350,000 hits already on Youtube. An Internet flame war has erupted between feminists and Muslims and there's talk of copycat 'Champagne Slut' protests occurring in other major cities. Diplomats are getting twitchy. Embassies are being put on alert. The Israelis are chomping at the bit to get outraged but can't quite decide whether Casey's 'statement' was anti-Semitic or anti-Muslim, both or neither. As a politician, she'd go far – the Minister for Women and Equalities would be proud. It's like World War Z, but - you know, where both sides are bearded, twitter savvy, attack zombies.

I've got a feeling this meeting is not going to be quick. On the way to Dr Jones's office Maria falls into step beside me.

'You should see this Meester Waxman,' she tells me earnestly, pointing to her phone.

'No I shouldn't Maria,' I tell her.

Maria has been monitoring 'communications' since the SlutWalk and against my express wishes has insisted on keeping me up to date with every twist and turn of the twatter traffic. Did I say twatter? What I meant was twatter.

I leave her at the entrance of the HR department waving her phone at me, trying to show me the latest tweets. Dr Jones's office is at the far end of a cubicle farm and I have to walk a gauntlet of staring eyes and public sector approved screen savers, telling me:

'Be true to your work, your word, and your friends.'

Another telling me: 'Never look back unless you are planning to go that way.'

A tea mug telling me: 'It is never too late to give up our prejudices.'

These people with no life or ambition reducing Thoreau and Emerson to a drop down menu of life affirming quotes that somehow expresses how they want the world to view them. It's really, really depressing. Seriously, someone needs to call the fucking context police.

Dr Jones's secretary dips her head to look at me above her half moon glasses like some old school ma'am then, after a brief interlude that is supposed to communicate something like, 'I am Cerberus, the gatekeeper of hell!' she waves me to the door without a word.

Inside, Dr Jones is sat at his desk, hands firmly clasped around a coffee mug which has a photo of his kids printed on it; a birthday present from his wife no doubt. He hasn't left the office since the fateful meeting and he looks like shit. Smiling nervously he stands up.

'These gentlemen would like a word with both of us,' he says, gouging at the bandages wrapped around his neck and nodding towards the two guys with matching black trench coats.

They both stand up and show me their badges and don't slap cuffs on me, which almost makes me cry with relief. But I don't cry. Like a man I sit down in the chair offered and merely whimper.

'I'm Detective Inspector Blackmore and this is my colleague Detective Sergeant Simpson,' says the one with a hair line working it's way to the back of his skull.

'Do you know why we're here Mr Waxman?'

I shake my head.

'I don't think I've done anything illegal,' I say, blinking innocently and hoping to God no-one asks for a urine sample.

The other one, the Detective Sergeant with the slicked back hair smirks.

'How about the little.. Mardi Gras you had the other day.'

'Er, maybe,' I tell him.

'Maybe?'

'Maybe I had a little accident.'

'Accident?'

'With some champagne.'

'Champagne?'

Fuck me, is he going to repeat everything I say? I need to be careful here; one wrong word and I'm toast.

After decades of kicking the crap out of minorities, the police are a little over-compensatory these days; a bit like reformed smokers – I wouldn't be surprised if they even have a couple of WPO's on the SlutWalk next year.

I spell it out for him as slowly and carefully as I can, with as few references to race, religion, sexual orientation or gender as I can possibly get.

'I may have.. inadvertently.. spilt some champagne on some.. person's erm.. jubbah.. by accident.'

Both of them square their shoulders.

'Mr Waxman,' says the DI, tilting his head menacingly at me.

'May I remind you that using racist terms is an arrestable offence under the Public Order Act!'

'What racist term?' I ask him panicked.

'Jubbah,' he bunny fingers at me ominously.

'Jubbah isn't racist!' I tell him.

'It doesn't have to BE racist Mr Waxman,' the DS interrupts, eager to put his equality and diversity training to use. 'By law, if it is merely PERCEIVED to be racist by the victim or any other person, then it IS racist.'

Perceived? You've got to be shitting me?

'But a jubbah is what people of a - you know, Muslims persuasion WEAR. I spilt some champagne on someone's item of clothing.. by accident!'

Dickhead.

'Oh I see,' says the DI.

Then there's some laughing about something that's not really funny for a long time which ends in a sort of.. hmmm.

'Anyway, it's not 'ethnic minority,' it's 'minority ethnic." I inform him helpfully.

'What is?'

'The term for - you know, 'ethnic minorities."

'No shit?' he says, genuinely surprised. 'I must have missed that one.'

'Yeah, I got the memo this morning,' I tell him.

Pause

'You get them too huh?' he asks.

We both of us nod, and there's that special melancholic silence that passes between two war weary veterans that have shared too much in the horrors and brutality of conflict. We're bonding, I can feel it.

'Can I offer anyone tea?' asks Dr Jones.

'Probably a good idea,' says the DI, taking charge again and pacing the floor. 'We have a few logistics to discuss and it may take some time.'

He walks over to the window and narrows his eyes at the car park, probably trying to see his car in the distance if the obese women from estates had anything to do with the parking arrangements.

'Sandra,' says Dr Jones into the intercom. 'Could we possibly arrange some tea for the gentlemen please?'

There's a crackle of static and a pause. Then Sandra's

clipped voice comes back.

'I am an administrative assistant Dr Jones: a person, whose work consists of supporting management, using a variety of project management, communication and organisational skills. My job description does not include tea making.'

Then another crackle of static and silence. Through the flimsy door of the office we hear the slap, slapping of a high fives.

'Ouch, you told HIM Sandra.'

Another,

'Ohhhh, that put that sexist pig in his place.'

Another Pause.

'Erm.. thank you Sandra,' he says amicably into the dead air of the intercom, beginning to tear at his bandages once again.

The DI clears his throat.

'I wasn't that thirsty anyway to be honest,' he says diplomatically, trying to inject some dignity back into proceedings.

'We're with Special Branch,' he says, moving swiftly on. 'Counter Terrorism to be precise. We deal with matters of national security and domestic extremism and have reason to believe that the college could be a target for Islamic fundamentalists.'

'Good God, why?' asks Dr Jones, suddenly alarmed.

'We have an extremely prominent equality statement on the front page of our website and our prospectus is very representative of all minorities!'

The DI looks at Dr Jones, then to me, and back to Dr Jones.

'Yeah, I don't really think that's going to cut it on this occasion sir,' says the DI.

'Surely you follow social media, working with students and all?'

'Actually Bill,' interrupts the DS, giving me a companionable nod and loading his bunny fingering. 'It's 'learners.''

'Actually they're 'stakeholders',' says Dr Jones irritably, seizing the opportunity to reclaim some self respect.

'And I still prefer to get MY news from reliable unbiased sources,' he tells us. 'Like the Guardian and BBC.'

The inspector looks at me and clears his throat again.

'Well anyway, thanks to Mr Waxman's little jamboree, GCHQ has informed us that intercepted communications indicate a low grade but credible threat to the college. We obviously have to take any threat of this nature seriously so I'm afraid some of my officers will be stationed around the college for a while. They'll be as discrete as possible of course, but I'm afraid Mr Waxman will have to take a short leave of absence.'

'Leave of absence?' asks Dr Jones horrified.

'We're short staffed as it is. There's a lot of illness going around; why does he need a leave of absence?'

'You mean I'm PERSONALLY being targeted by Islamic extremists?!' I interrupt - the penny finally dropping.

'Erm.. in a word, yes,' the DI tells me straight.

That's it; the pigeons have come home to roost, put their feet up in front of the TV and sent out for pizza.

I'm going to die.

'Emotions are running a little high at the moment Mr Waxman,' says the DI. 'It might be prudent for you to step out of routine for a while; find somewhere else to stay - you know, until we can identify the source of the threat and try to neutralise it.'

'For how long?' I ask him, not unduly unhappy at the prospect, it has to be said.

'You should be able to return to a relatively normal routine after the weekend, when we have appropriate security arrangements in place.'

'Well that's fortunate,' adds Dr Jones helpfully. 'At least you'll be back in time to defend yourself at the disciplinary hearing next week!'

'Er.. yeah, that's right Dr Jones.'

Wanker.

'In the meantime, the Detective Sergeant here will drive you home to collect any things you may need, then on to somewhere where you feel you'll be safest,' says the DI

'How serious is this threat? I mean, isn't it just trolls mouthing off over social media?' I ask the DI hopefully.

What I'm looking for here is a shrug of the shoulders and a, 'most probably.' What I get is him tapping at his phone before holding it up to my face.

'This was uploaded to Youtube this morning from Somalia,' he tells me, as a grainy figure in combat fatigues and a black hood buffers onto the screen, holding a Kalashnikoff.

'I call upon you today through the teachings of Islam, especially the brothers of Tower Hamlets who are like, in the city what I was born in … I call upon you to come to jihad, and cut the throat of the disbeliever Carl Waxman for like, humiliating our Muslim brothers innit?'

Yes the video is of poor quality; yes the production values are bad and the sound and lighting leaves a hell of a lot to be desired, but the message is pretty fucking unmistakable. The pen may be mightier than the sword, but no multi ethnic prospectus or equality statement, no matter how succinctly eulogised or euphemised is going to stop some psychopath from attempting to use my head as a fucking clutch bag.

'He doesn't sound very Somalian,' says Dr Jones, insightfully.

The DI shrugs.

'Yeh, one of Choudary's lot I shouldn't wonder. We do find that a lot of these nut-jobs have actually been educated in Britain.'

'Nut-job is hardly a politically correct term to be using Detective Inspector,' scolds Dr Jones, giving the DI a stern stare.

That's right Inspector. It's OK for some jihadist nutter to express a sincere desire to commit unthinkable atrocities to my collar measurement; it's fine for our education system to churn out inarticulate, sociopathic dumbfucks, who's idea of 'death or victory' is a choice between suicide bombing and the final of x-factor, but God forbid we should damage their self esteem. Clearly that would undermine their dignity and underlying vulnerability.

[They train young men to drop fire on people. But their commanders won't allow them to write 'fuck' on their airplanes because it is obscene.]

'It's 'mentally challenged,"' corrects Dr Jones.

He's not wrong there; it's fucking deranged.

*

The DS, my temporary 'protection' and appointed driver, escorts me back to the office, where Henry watches us in silence from his laptop, no doubt fully updated on my newly found Internet notoriety by Maria. I just can't bring myself to look at him since the disabled toilet incident with Hilary. Seriously, what do you say to someone who's got a cock like a baby's arm?

'You thought of somewhere to stay yet?' asks the DS, as I collect my jacket and bag from the back of a chair. 'B&B

maybe?' he offers.

I shake my head. More expense I do not need.

'I'll think of somewhere,' I tell him.

'You can stay at mine,' offers Henry reaching out to me in my hour of need and probably grateful I haven't reported his little fiesta with Hilary in the disabled toilets.

'I'm taking the kids off for the weekend. I'll need to swing by the old place after work to pick up a few things but after that, you can have it to yourself till Monday. I could pick you up and give you a lift back to work then if you like?'

'Perfect,' says the DS, shrugging and looking at me for confirmation.

When Henry's wife kicked him out of the family home, he moved onto the leaky, 30' wooden boat, his Dad had left him. It had been sitting on the mud in Newhaven harbour, neglected for the best part of two years when he turned up with his life in a suitcase and balls in his hand.

Damp and small as it was, it became his home for all of six months until his wife's divorce brief got wind of it and persuaded the judge to lump it in with her part of the settlement. The bitch ebayed it two weeks later, well below it's market value and pissed off to Thailand with Henry's builder on the proceeds 'to get over the divorce.' Which is when he moved into the flee pit that he now calls home. I learned all this over 'icebreaking' drinks at an end of term session down the local pub.

His kids rarely visit because his wi-fi connection is too slow for them to stream detractors to take their minds off the fact that just looking at the place brings them out in ring worm. So on the rare occasions he gets to exercise his visitation schedule, like when his wife goes on one of her spa breaks, 'to get some space,' he takes them off on weekend trips with whatever vouchers he can scrape together because most of his money goes on maintenance payments. It's what the family court's call an 'amicable settlement'

'Yeah, perfect. Er, thanks Henry,' I tell him, while all the time thinking, YOU'VE GOT A MONSTER COCK!

He hands me his spare keys, WITH HIS MONSTER COCK HANDS! and an address on a postit, and the DS escorts me to his car.

As we're pulling out of the car park Jeremy waves us down with a wad of papers. I open the window and he pushes them at me with a pen.

'You need to sign these,' he tells me breathlessly. 'I've already talked to your psychiatrist at the hospital but I need access to your medical records for the disciplinary hearing next week. I think they may help with your defence.'

What the hell. I sign, then signal for the DS to take me home.

22 WORKING WITH GROUPS AND INDIVIDUALS

I open the door to my apartment and step around the letters from the banks, finance companies and debt collection agencies that I've been ignoring for the last few days. Tentatively, I poke the pile with my toe to check there's no letter bombs or suspicious looking parcels. I flick on my Samsung 57" for some background noise and a bit of a misdirect, as I quickly clear the old credit card and mirror from the coffee table. A few years ago I'd have parties here that made the Wolf of Wall Street look like a nursery school Christmas party.

Not now.

Not any more.

The DS looks around the place, runs a hand over the Cococucine Italian kitchen surface, takes a piss in my Villeroy and Boch toilet and is clearly admiring the exceptionally light and spacious interior. He wanders onto the balcony to take in the panoramic views of Croydon. The question on his lips is, 'Where did you get the money for this?!' Which is perhaps not something you'd want a copper to be asking himself.

I throw a few things into an overnight bag - no need to change or overdo the packing as I'll be back on Monday. I shout to the DS that I'm ready and he comes in from the balcony, looks at me and frowns. Granted I'm not dressed to kill but he's hardly Mr GQ himself, in his police issue flasher's mac.

'You not changing for your hot date tonight then?' he says.

'Date?'

'It's on your wall calendar.'

He points to the calendar with the word 'DATE' scrawled across it.

facepalm

And here's another cunt who clearly doesn't miss a trick.

I admit, in all the excitement I'd forgotten about meeting up with Rachel tonight. As a rule I don't 'date,' but circumstances dictate that Rachel and I are now officially being 'exclusive' as she puts it, as a prelude to being engaged and slaughtered as a blood sacrifice on the altar of marriage.

I go back into the bedroom and take a quick shower and change into my B-Side by Wale panelled t-shirt with a James Long mesh neoprene bomber jacket which I would normally wear with my Balmain classic mid-rise jeans - slim leg obviously, but lately my balls are deferring to the Dolce and Gabbana cotton jersey jogging trousers.. Granted, the look is a bit 'Russian Mafia,' but hey, they're clean so they should see me through for work on Monday too.

Why am I even bothering with this charade anyway? The little 'dating' I've done merely reinforces my theory that 'dates' are just a platform for women to talk about themselves ad nauseam, until men have punctuated the tedium with enough complements to get to sex. There is however no guarantee of sex, so it becomes a soul destroying waiting game of chance. That's why the brevity, clarity, honesty and downright value for money of prostitution will always trump the hypocrisy of dating. The reason why so many feminists demand a clampdown on prostitution is so men will be forced into restaurants to listen to them bang on about their 'issues' while tucking into a free meal. It's the only way they can get themselves heard, and just another way to torment, demean and undermine men. They'll probably want to start with a bloody 'icebreaker' too.

Most women are their own favourite subject and could talk for hours about themselves, their friends and... themselves again. The greatest compliment a woman can bestow on a man is that he's a 'good listener.' A 'good listener' means a women gets to yack on even more about herself than you'd think was humanly possible. Luckily, where women are born to talk, men have evolved the ability to ignore; it's part of a man's evolutionary DNA, but also why so many feminist policies get sneaked through parliament without anyone noticing until something like Birmingham's, 'equal value' fiasco blows up in your face, costing the tax payer fucking billions.

Luckily on this occasion, Rachel's mother has conceded

that we may need some 'personal' time together, without her chaperoning services. All the same, a cinema 'date' has an overriding advantage, in that there is little talking involved. And without her mother in the way, it may give me an opportunity to bring her to her senses, or at least plant some seeds of doubt in her mind about the whole fucking debacle of this 'relationship.'

Marriage opt outs I've considered so far, apart from faking the brain aneurism are:

- Emigration
- Suicide
- Catching homosexuality

The best lies however, are those with a toe dipped in the cool waters of truth. I figure when she catches sight of the state my balls are in, I'll 'reluctantly' recount some recent fictitious war story, (maybe I saved a puppy from drowning or something) that has resulted in my chronic infertility. This will no doubt filter back to her mother who, being primarily motivated by grandchildren will release me from any matrimonial obligation while simultaneously being sufficiently sympathetic to my condition to drop the rape allegations.

Genius?

Damned right.

I will of course be 'devastated' at the demise of our engagement and offer increasingly desperate suggestions to safeguard our future together. We could engage the services of an adoption agency, I'll implore, or perhaps a sperm donor clinic? This will merely accelerate the breakup of our fledgling relationship, because if there's one thing teaching has taught me, is that there's nothing more pathetic and depressing than an eager underachiever.

On the other hand, there's always an outside chance she'll go for the sperm donor option on account of them all being Phd's and Nobel prize winners, so maybe I shouldn't over egg the pudding so to speak, and just let nature take it's course. Besides, I'm ideologically opposed to sperm donor clinics on evolutionary, legal and moral grounds because it means women like Carol get to perpetuate their genes.

In the 9th Century, raiding parties of Vikings raped and pillaged their way through Northumbria and Yorkshire, leaving a drunken trail of illegitimate babies in their wake. Cute as these babies were, this possibly wasn't the most politically correct way in which to leave your mark on the gene pool and on Saturday nights, this unfortunate genetic legacy is still evident in contemporary North-eastern towns.

Similarly, sperm donor clinics were invented by feminists as a way of raping and pillaging their way into the gene pool, because no man in their right mind would have voluntary sex with a sascrotch like Carol, unless of course it's a man-feminist and would in any case suffer from extremely low sperm count. (A man-feminist is like a male praying mantis, in that he is so desperate to get laid, that he will quite literally allow his head to be chewed off in order to have sex).

Yes literally.

Sperm donation is like Darwinian Rohypnol, and should be illegal.

I don't know why it's not.

The irony of sperm donations however, is that when these radical feminists started knocking themselves up from intelligent, test tube sperm in the 60's and 70', all they were doing was procreating a legion of little knuckle babies with high IQs, genetically predisposed to saucing their tacos in darkened rooms to hard-core porn. That's why, when the first 'sperm donor' babies reached their fourteenth birthday, they immediately raced for their bedrooms, keyboard in one hand, raging spunk trumpet in the other and knocked out the entire fucking Internet porn industry in an afternoon.

As grateful as I am for these unintended consequences, it's just not natural.

'Ready now?' asks the DS.

'One last thing,' I tell him, and I tease the 'Apocalypse Now - Redux version ' DVD from the stack.

'Nice,' he tells me on seeing it. 'What's your favourite scene?'

'Death from above, yours?'

'Kilgore on the beach.'

'Sweet.'

We're still deep in discussing Coppola's masterpiece, as we leave the car park, but the sight of some Asian guy hanging around the gates gets him refocused, and he radios for some goons to go check him out, and my paranoia returns with a vengeance.

'Don't you guys do relocation programs?' I ask the DS. 'You know, change people's identity and that sort of thing?'

He looks at me with a rye smile.

'I think it's a bit early in the day to be thinking about that sort of thing. No offence, but you're not exactly Salman fucking Rushdie,' he tells me with a laugh.

Tosser.

Fatwa or no fatwa, a change of identity and relocation could solve a lot of problems for me. So I push the issue.

'What about a little plastic surgery?'

'We don't really endorse it,' he informs me, with a hint of irritation creeping into his voice.

By the time the DS drops me at Henry's address it's not even Midday. He gives me his mobile number in case of emergencies then I let myself in. The contrast with my place is.. decidedly manifest. What the hell keeps him from reaching for the pill bottle at night as he stares at the peeling linoleum and yellowing paint, rocking himself to sleep? And I'm thinking, how long will it be before I'm trawling the Friday adds for a cesspit like this?

Quickly dumping the bag, I head back out before I'm tempted to 'make myself comfortable' and head down the street, into Henry's neighbourhood to find something to eat. I settle on some greasy spoon and sit in the corner alone, back to the wall, shivering and mindful of my predicament. I should have worn my John Smedley cashmere blend; I just wasn't thinking straight, although the thought of infusing it with the smell of bacon fat doesn't bear thinking about.

Some Eastern European waitress comes over, takes my order and quickly leaves. I'm off the Vitex now so enjoy the freedom of movement my Dolce and Gabbana's allow. I contemplate going for a quick smoke, but I still haven't warmed up from the short walk here, so there's no way I'm going back outside to stand in a freezing, piss soaked doorway to exercise my God given human right to cancer. The smoking ban might have prevented a few secondary carcinomas, but it's probably killed off a whole fucking generation with hypothermia and exposure. Despite a ban on smoking, mercifully the licensing laws have gone the other way, so I order a couple of vodka chasers to wash down the all day breakfast.

I'm mopping up the last of the bean juice with synthetic white bread when some middle-age Asian scrubber comes in and sits at the table opposite. Despite the temperature she's only got a mini skirt covering the broken veins on her legs and a McKenzie tracksuit top for warmth. Given that Geordies rarely venture this far south, I'm guessing she's some local perma-fried crack whore. But if there's one thing I learnt from a SlutWalk banner however, it's not to judge anyone by the way they dress.

I notice she has a rollup behind her ear, so lean over to ask if I can borrow some cigarette papers. She tells me she's £50 a turn or £140 an hour.

As if.

She's obviously clocked the threads I'm wearing and trying her luck, and I learn a valuable life lesson. Never believe a slut with a banner.

I pay the waitress and leave, but as I wander down the street I begin to realise that there's not much in the way of legal entertainment and resort to browsing a newsagent/post-office for something to read. The selection isn't great. There are three 'lads mags', for your unreconstructed wannabe, wrapped in opaque cellophane on the top shelf tucked out of sight, like they're ground zero for the H7N9 virus. I really don't know what the problem is, I've spanked the monkey to more fashion magazines and lingerie catalogues than I ever have to lads mags.

Being so high and inaccessible, they are surely contravening the rights of short men too. I should write to my local MP about it.

No porn of course.

That would be sexist.

No matter, looking further down the rack, the female form is being viciously judged anyway by a raft of women's magazines, whose whole raison d'être, as far as I can tell, is the blatant objectification and shaming of women. Beside them are TV guides, astrological magazines, new age magazines and yet more women's magazines.

And more.

Features like 'Top ten vibrators tested!' 'How to seduce a millionaire!' 'My three hour orgasm!' Articles on fashion and yet more last 'taboos' that women are apparently afraid to discuss. I haven't met a woman yet afraid to discuss anything at great length and in colossal detail, as proven by the immense range of these shit magazines. There's some gay magazines too with covers of the topless Simon and Nigel chillaxing without the aid of any cellophane censorship, their thumbs suggestively hooked in each other's briefs, which just goes to prove yet again that objectification of the body is merely a natural part of the male sexual arousal process and nothing to do with misogyny.

I'm looking at you, Carol.

I move across to the book section. Apart from the insipid James Patterson collective, it's floor to ceiling chiclit and celebrity chefs. It's like some modern art display depicting the lesbian bed death of the publishing industry. If we binned that lot we could save about a million trees and free up precious shelf space for Andy McNabb or any other books that don't have an Oprah fucking Winfrey endorsement. EL James has almost got an entire 'erotica literature' section to herself. I blame EL James for the likes of Svetlana by raising the benchmark of women's expectation in relation to sadomasochism. If only Joseph Fritzel had been a sharp suited multi millionaire, he wouldn't be languishing in jail right now, he'd be a 'mummy porn' phenomenon.

But he isn't.

There's an entire section dedicated to 'Self Help.' And you've got to ask yourself who reads that sort of crap? Besides, 'Self Help' books can all be summed up in one sentence, bereft of any of the euphemistic bollocks that you'd never read anyway.

'Quit smoking you fat freak and sort your shit out because nobody likes you!'

That'll be £7.99 you insecure, ineffectual aberration.

I buy a paper with tits in it, not because there's anything

worth reading, just on principal. I then pop next door to the off licence where I purchase some cigarette papers and a bottle of 'on offer' gin, figuring on a spot of light prinking before tonight's date with Rachel.

I find a bench and take a sly glug from the bottle, watching people going about their business; shoving push chairs, arguing on phones and freaking me out with their suspicious glances and pitiful stares. Where's a bomb scare when you really need one?

Some dosser sidles up to me and offers me suck on his tin of Tennent's Super. It's like public transport except - you know, without going anywhere. Then I catch sight of my reflection in a shop window, and I have to ask myself.

- A lot of questions

In education we call this 'reflective practice', but again it's not something that I'm comfortable with. I don't even know why I mentioned it.

So I ignore the self-reflection and self-medicate on a large slurp of the proffered tramp juice instead.

23 SAFEGUARDING

I guess if I had to fight off a frenzied machete attack from a psychotic terrorist, I could always deploy Rachel as a body shield, or use her to cushion the explosion from a ticking rucksack, giving me an opportunity to turn and run, thus solving both the immediate threat to my life and the long term risk to my freedom. It's win-win when you think about it.

Buoyed by these heroic thoughts as I am, I'm still having sporadic nervous breakdowns every time I see anyone resembling a Muslim - I should never have mixed that gin with tramp juice. Not all Muslims are terrorists it's true - a lot less than 90% by all accounts, but all Islamic terrorists I've ever heard of are Muslim and that's the angle my paranoia is going with, no matter what the bloody Equality Act tells me to think.

The Equality Act of course, makes the 1984 'Thought Police' training manual look like a Sunday school pamphlet; it's so invasive and all encompassing, you could wear it as a stab jacket when the resulting red-tape shortage riots kick off.

Every time I walk through a door there's a moment of trepidation, while I scan the room and ready my karate moves like I'm Inspector fucking Clouseau.

'What are you doing?' asks Rachel as we enter the cinema.

'Erm.. checking the best line of sight for the film,' I tell her, pointing to a far corner. 'Over there seems good.'

'You're funny,' she informs me.

Granted, a girl used to the best restaurants and clubs in London is hardly going to be that enamoured with Cineworld, but I'm not out to impress; I'm out to survive, and a dark cinema surrounded by young couples and families, or 'human shields' as I like to regard them, seems as good an option as any. We manage to sit down at the back of the cinema, in a corner near the fire exit without being assassinated. Rachel is blissfully unaware that I'm freaking out throughout the entire film, anticipating some Colorado style multiplex massacre, and paying little attention to the screen.

The film (as far as I can tell) is some girl power empowerment propaganda, where a near naked girl with skinny arms and a bow.. and an inexhaustible supply of arrows, defeats an evil patriarchal elite that has infinitely superior fire-power in a dystopian future.

When it comes to the obligatory, post film critique in the bar afterwards (I'm resigned to the fact that there has to be talking at some point), I've got nothing to contribute to the conversation other than what I remember from the reviews earlier in the week. Not that it matters anyway, because as she reminds me, I'm a 'good listener.'

I notice as I'm 'listening' that she has a slightly sticky out chin. The type of thing that in the early stages of a relationship you might tweak and think was endearing and even miss when you're not together. But over the course of the relationship it would become increasingly irritating as she jabs it in your face when reminding you not to leave wet towels on the bed, or not to piss all over the toilet seat (why does domestic bathroom furniture only cater to a woman's anatomy? Install urinals for fuck sake)! After a while it'd be the only damn thing you notice about her.

That chin.

It would encapsulate and represent all that was wrong with the relationship and all that you despise about her. And long after you've split the house into a 10%/90% equal share, lost custody of the kids, handed over all your money in maintenance payments in an amicable, family court imposed agreement, you'll be sharing a warm can of special brew on a piss-stained bench in the park and it'll be the only damn thing you can think about.

That fucking deformed, sticky-out mutant chin of hers.

I nod, listen, drink and look at her chin, until mercifully her phone rings and she takes it outside where there's better reception. I move our drinks to the over stuffed Winchester sofa in the corner with it's sturdy back against an even sturdier wall with a better view of the room. I have become Jason Bourne. I ease myself onto the soft cushion of the sofa and begin mine sweeping the dregs left on the table by the previous occupiers in another value-for-money attempt to numb the mental and physical pain.

But then I spot it.

A little cellophane bag of coloured pills, no more than four or five just about to work their way down the back of the sofa. I whip them up in one fluid movement and look around to see if anyone's noticed.

Nope.

Rachel is still pacing up and down the pavement outside, deep in conversation, so I retrieve a couple and knock them back with my stupidly expensive Belgian beer that she paid for (thank-you feminism) and slip the rest in my back pocket.

Later in the evening, when I judge the time is right to have earned enough sex credit (or bitchcoin as I like to term it), I'll suggest going back to Henry's place. Again, I'm not out to impress here. We'll have sex, then, perhaps during some uncompromising tea bagging session she'll comment on my ball, or lack thereof, and it's then I'll dump my infertility bombshell on her and hopefully wipe the slate clean.

So to speak.

Rachel returns, and sits next to me, hooks an arm around mine and nuzzles her head under my chin

'Mummy sends her love,' she says, as if we're the fucking Waltons or something.

'She was asking when you're going to propose. She says she needs a date in the diary and what's the point of hanging about?'

'I er.. I haven't even got the ring yet. I wanted to do things properly; one knee and all that stuff, you know?'

'Don't upset her Carl,' she warns me ominously. 'Mummy can be quite the dragon when she wants to be. Honestly, you have no idea.'

No shit.

'God, think of ME in a wedding dress though; in front of all those people?!'

I do Rachel, I do. It gives me the tremours and brings me out in a cold sweat.

'Do you love me, Carl?' she asks out of the blue.

Say what?! Where did that shit come from?

'What? What do you mean; do I love you? I er.. I mean we're getting engaged aren't we?'

She purrs and nuzzles in even closer.

What is it about this, 'I love you' shit that makes a woman act like she's just washed down a handful of benzodiazepines after prolonged electroconvulsive treatment? You can be in a fight to the death, but throw in, 'but I love you' at the opportune moment and bam! She retracts her claws and 'make-up sex' is on the cards, as sure as night follows day.

It's not like it even means anything. Hell, I loved my car with all my heart, truly I did, but as soon as a newer, stylish model came out I was down the showroom and all over it like a fucking rash. I was waxing the smurf over pictures of it on the Internet long before that. I wanted it more than life itself. It didn't mean I loved my old car any less - I wasn't lying to Svetlana when I said it had sentimental value - but if I'd had the money I would have traded it in for the newer model in a heartbeat. Commitment and sentimental value is something poor people have when they can't afford new shit. When was the last time you saw a millionaire with a shit car and ugly girlfriend?

Exactly.

'You know,' she says, deciding to 'share.' 'I've never understood those girls who are all career driven: those feminists who want to be the same as men. It's so, unattractive don't you think?'

I take a slug of beer, seeing maybe a glimmer of light.

'Well I suppose some women get a lot of satisfaction out of that sort of thing, and why not? This is the 21st century after all and some men find pushy, ambitious women.. captivating.' I tell her, supporting a woman's natural right to self-determination, equality and being unappealing.

'Rachel,' I say, taking her hands in mine and looking directly into her eyes. 'I would support you 110% if you perhaps - you know, decided to pursue a career before deciding to settle down with me. No matter how long it would take.'

She pulls back and looks at me quizzically, and for a moment my heart stops. Then she returns to her nuzzling.

'You're so modern and.. metrosexual Carl.'

Eugh, I feel soiled! I feel grubby and impure, befouled and begrimed.

'I have to go to the toilet,' I tell her - I have to puke is what I really need to do.

'Be careful not to use the 'T' word around Daddy,' she warns me as I get up. 'It's 'bathroom' OK?'

In the 'bathroom' that has no bath (fucking Americans), I take the urinal close to the door. There are five urinals in total, and it is a truth universally acknowledged that the next user should leave at least one urinal between me and him and under no circumstances, speak. When both of these universal laws are broken simultaneously, the natural order of things breaks down and Bruce Willis needs to be called.

'You Carl Waxman?' says the large Asian bloke suddenly appearing next to me.

I've never met this guy before in my life.. except.. except when he was hanging around my apartment gates earlier. He's too old to be a student and he's got a small rucksack hanging over one shoulder.

Fuck.

Seeing the almighty gush of piss that comes out of me, confirms to him that he has found his prey. He reaches into his pocket but I don't wait. I've been like a coiled spring all day, and now with a few drinks and indeterminate drugs inside me, I'm feeling emboldened and remorseless. I get the first move in quick, with a karate chop to his neck that completely misses the target. He flinches.

'What are you doing?' he asks rubbing his shoulder.

Plan B is to run. Running was really plan A all along if the truth be told, I don't know what the fuck I was thinking with the karate chop. I've never been any good at that sort of thing. I bolt for the door with the nub of my cock still hanging out.

As I leg it past Rachel I waggle my pinkie and thumb at her in a phone gesture.

'I'll call you later, OK?'

Then burst out of the door and away down the street, thinking perhaps, he may decide against a pointless pursuit (seeing how fast I can run) and kidnap Rachel instead. Cowardice, when done in the right way, can be very cathartic

[Run, Charlie!]

Kidnapping Rachel would be fine. I could play the fraught fiancé in tears, begging for the terrorists to spare my beloved's life on live TV. Then I could cut an exclusive deal with one of the tabloids and they would be there to record how distraught I'd be when the severed ear turned up. I would beg the government to do something, anything, but they would say they don't make deals with terrorists and would attract embarrassingly low ratings for themselves. Her parents are rich so they would make a behind the scenes deal via a shady third party negotiator and she would be released.

At the press conference I would hug her and say how relieved I was to have her back in my life and I always knew in my heart of hearts that she would be delivered to me safe eventually, except for the missing ear of course. They can do wonderful things with surgery these days. Perhaps they could do something with that fucking chin too while they're at it. I would be brave, with tears in my eyes and write a book and share my 'secret' anguish on several cross media platforms, across all territories, the film rights alone paying for a top society wedding and messy divorce which would be covered by OK magazine and other glossies, who I'd sue for intrusion of privacy. I'd then start dating a top Russian lingerie model who wouldn't speak English and I wouldn't speak Russian so we would just have sex all the time and that would be fine, because finally I would have found the spiritual happiness and contentment I didn't realise I was actually looking for all along, Oprah.

Furthermore, I wouldn't need Maslow's pyramid of fucking hierarchical needs to tell me that being ball deep in a Russian lingerie model would embody the whole concept of 'self actualising.'

I run and run through dark streets and deserted alleys, until I'm totally lost. Then run some more. I slow to a kind of race-walk pace when the phone rings and I see Rachel's name on my screen. I contemplate not answering it at first; I didn't expect negotiations to start this soon, so I climb into a builder's skip and hunker down.

'Where did you go?' she asks, sounding pissed off.

'Don't panic Rachel I'm here for you,' I tell her, being brave and manly, while making sneaky whack-a-mole peaks over the top of the skip to check I haven't been tailed.

There's a pause.

'You're acting weird Carl. Mummy told me this would happen; she said it happens to all men before they get married.'

'Let me talk to the terrorists,' I demand. 'Tell them I will not be manipulated by this emotional blackmail!'

'Carl this is not funny. I'm bored, I'm tired and I've had a very odd conversation with some tabloid journalist, who's told me some disturbing things about you. I'm going home. I suggest you do the same. Mummy will hear of this.'

Rachel, my beloved life's ruin, lets the implied threat sink in, then hangs up and all my hopes and dreams of dating a top Russian lingerie model evaporate, which makes me feel very depressed and emotional. I lie back on the skip's inevitable mattress and stare up at the sodium sky, tears filling my eyes. Into the dead air of the phone I tell her.

'Hope in reality is the worst of all evils because it prolongs the torment of man.'

You can't beat a bit of Nietzsche for a little light-hearted cosmic purposelessness and existential hopelessness. I lie there for I don't know how long, listening to the relentless buzz of the city traffic and the twenty-four hour party people on riverboats traversing the Thames. Waiting, waiting for some Coppola-esce inspiration to carry me through the depths of despair and onto greatness. In the distance, I hear another sound - the faint sound of music coming from some theatre on South Bank.

I watch helicopters clatter slowly overhead; bankers, executives and oligarchs being ferried around from yachts to venues to office blocks to football stadiums, looking down on us mere mortals and getting blown by top of the range, tax free hookers.

Quietly at first, but soon the brass section of Wagner's, Ride of the Valkyries fills the night sky. I sit up slowly, aware of someone standing on the mattress beside me, silhouetted against the refracted light of the Thames. He looks up at the helicopters and touches the brim of his ten gallon hat while casually chewing on his gum. The music ramps up even higher. Behind him, the embankment suddenly lights up in a blaze of orange brilliance, and the roar in my ears is deafening. He doesn't recoil; he doesn't react at all, just kneels and takes a deep lungful of air as if.. well as if nothing in the world smells like that.

'Charlie Whiskey?' says Lieutenant Colonel Kilgore, looking down at me and reaching out a hand. 'Shall we dance?'

24 PLANNING FOR ASSESSMENT

Dawn is breaking when I finally find myself back at Henry's flat, with no recollection of how I got there. Kilgore has left the party and the comedown is kicking in. By the time I finally manage to stab the key in the lock, my pizza is hanging out of its box and a vodka bottle lies smashed on the step. Even taking in to account my chemically inconvenienced state, this place is still fucking grim. Any time soon Henry's kids will be off to university where Henry will be called upon to cough up even more money to finance a whole other pile of shit under the guise of 'education' that they'll just end up pissing against the wall before taking a soul destroying job in a cubical farm. It will also necessitate Henry's prolonged stay in this shit hole until well after retirement. Surely even he can see the pointlessness of it all?

'As long as the kids are happy, that's the main thing.'

That'll be his bloody epitaph.

After a clamorous search of the cupboards I unearth an

eclectic mix of tequila and Jaegermeister miniatures and a litre of Hendricks gin. I kick off my shoes and jacket then lie on the bed, planning to lose the rest of the weekend to self-pity and abuse. I roll myself a calamitous mooter with skins sticking out at all angles. Come Tuesday, at best I'll be queuing behind Burberry caps at the dole office, or at worst, doing face time with a swab and rap sheet at the local nick.

Rock bottom.

I turn on the TV at the foot of the bed for company and flick between the porn channels, which all show looping commercials of what you could have if you only had the subscription. I mean here's a single bloke in his 50's living on his own - AND NO PORN SUBSCRIPTION! What's all that about?

I root through my bag and tease out 'Apocalypse Now - Redux'. I push it into the DVD player and watch the opening scene of Vietnam being napalmed to the sound of the Doors, which always calms me and brings me back to some measure of equilibrium. To think this piece of cinematic gold was pulled from the cutting room bin by Coppola himself fills me with redemptive hope.

Where the morning goes after that I have no idea but midday finds me pretzel'd in the bed sheets with my clothes still on and a half eaten pizza stuck to my face. The DVD has looped and voices of Kilgore and Kurts are still playing at some deeper subconscious in my dream feted head. Captain Willard is still telling me.

[Every minute I stay in this room, I get weaker, and every minute Charlie squats in the bush, he gets stronger.

> Each time I looked around, the walls
> moved in a little tighter.]

Empty miniatures litter the floor and my one remaining ball is throbbing so much I need to peel off my boxers very, very slowly in order to give it some relief. I finish off the rest of the pizza with some gin then fold myself back into the bed for a fitful afternoon of feverishly short sleeps.

A nightmare delivers me into the early evening in a cold sweat and a raging need to piss so I patter to the bathroom and the relief is immense and immediate. Next I take up a kneeling position on the cold, worn lino for spectacular bout of incredibly misdirected vomiting which necessitates me stripping off my sick spattered clothes and dumping them in the shower tray to ferment. It's then I notice my remaining ball has swollen to twice its normal size and taken on a curious shade of mauve. I pop another Oxycodone to quell the pain and wrap myself in Henry's dressing gown hanging on the back of the door. I drain the last of the gin then go back to sleep.

Come late evening it's dark and I wake up once more. I have no idea what the time is but I'm so hungry I try licking the fucking pizza box for nourishment. Eventually, I crawl out of bed, pull on the some of Henry's clean sweatpants I find in a drawer, give up looking for my second shoe which has mysteriously disappeared, and step into Henry's Crocs lying by the door.

Ten minutes later and I'm down the street, shuffling along the isle of a Tesco Metro in Henry's dressing gown looking like Jeff Lebowski's evil twin. I've got a four pack of rice pudding in one hand and a bottle of discounted Polish vodka in the other. At the self-service till I max out my overdraft limit with a £40 cash-back, before some mysterious direct debit I've failed to keep track of shafts it completely. Then it occurs to me that it's unusually quiet for a Saturday night. I look around, shivering and sweating like some radicalised ticking Muslim, wondering where all the fucking infidels have gone. The wall clock tells me it's 4:15am. I must have slept longer than I thought.

On the way back to the flat I catch the eye of the oriental Tom I saw at the cafe earlier, coming out of some bedsit, no doubt working the late shift. Who in God's name uses these middle aged, bargain basement hookers?

'Busy?' I ask, not quite knowing why; guess I'm just being polite.

'Rike noodle soup, sweety.' she says, stubbing out her discarded fag with the chipped heel of her stiletto. 'I go for rong, rong time. I no get tired. You rike massage?'

I shake my head. She makes a sad face that I'm guessing is supposed to be endearing, but just makes it look even more like a bag of smacked arses. It proves one thing though. It proves that there are still some professions that even women like this, with a strong work ethic can make a key contribution to the British economy despite her looks and lifestyle by simply monetizing sexual consent.

There are an estimated 80,000 sex workers in the UK, about the same as BP employs worldwide. Street prostitutes, who make up only about 10% of sex workers, can earn £10-£15 for ten minutes work, and that's your greasy, Mckenzie clad growler with heroine tracks and no teeth or education.

Moving up the career ladder, your average sauna masseuse is earning £40 - £50 a turn, and moving up even further an independent escort is on £200 with a minimum booking of three hours.

It doesn't stop there either.

A high class independent escort is charging £3000 a day or more, and for a high class 'courtesan' we're looking in the region of £5000 minimum plus tips and expenses. That's even more than a hedge fund manger with a part-time job in the premier league. You want to talk about role models for girls? There's your hard working, top earning elite right there, and girls have got more chance of 'self actualising' as an escort or courtesan than they ever have of becoming a cabinet minister or CEO, therefore diminishing the risk of depression in later life because of unrealistic expectations imposed on them by feminists.

Of course there is exploitation within sex work as there is with all industries and some will point to the evils of trafficking to vilify the profession. But let's face it, if there were a shortage of plumbers to the point they were charging 5K a job and criminal gangs were 'trafficking' them to fulfil demand, would there be calls for the plumbing profession to be outlawed?

Get real.

The government would be de-criminalising it, taxing it and encouraging the legions of unemployed to train up for these high demand, vital roles which would have the added bonus of bringing prices down to more affordable levels for Joe public. It doesn't take a socioeconomic genius to work that one out. The work is extremely family friendly as the hours are flexible and there's entry at every level. So to speak. Sex work is also very sociable as workers get to meet lots of interesting people because let's face it, there's Johns on every street corner needing their nads siphoned at least twice a day and there always will be. But more importantly from a feminist perspective, it's an industry dominated by women - 95% of sex workers are women and they are much better paid than their minority male colleagues.

It probably goes some way to explaining why feminists want it banned on the grounds it disproves every argument they have on the gender pay gap, discrimination, and equal and fair representation. It's an inconvenient truth that undermines their entire fucking raison d'être.

'Ahh, baby,' says the Tom, bringing her face up close to mine.

'Sure you no want me to rerax you?'

Rerax? Are you kidding me? Even in the state I'm in, there's no disguising the fact that her breath smells like a Cambodia fish cannery. I try shuffling away from her but her hand somehow snakes its way into Henry's sweatpants, locks on to my cock and starts massaging. And that right there is another case of serious sexual assault that will forever remain within the 'hidden statistics'.

It's a disgrace.

The police should be informed.

'Just fuck off.. er.. ple...'

Oh sweet Jesus, it does; it does feel good though. We stagger up the road for a few yards like some spastic pantomime horse at a Nuremberg rally, except with rice pudding and Crocs - Nazis would never go for that shit - before slowly, slowly like the horse whisperer, she tames the beast and I come to a stop. She leads me slowly by the cock into a doorway where she brings my lap cannon right up to the edge of the castle walls before stopping and whispering in my ear.

'You have prace around here sweety?'

Back at Henry's flat, we're half way through the vodka and she is frenzying away on my mutton batten to no effect whatsoever. She's already changed hands twice trying to coax the fucking thing back into some sort of re-useable state. Every time I get a whiff of her breath I'm instantly reminded of seafood, which is not helping. She unclips her immense bra sack with her free hand and her tit's splash down on to her pock marked belly in some misguided belief that this will somehow raise my sleeping beast.

It doesn't.

It really doesn't.

Worse, the Oxycodone has worn off and my pain threshold is about to go over its event horizon again, so I stop the charade. I pop another Oxycodone and we share a couple of benzodiazepines she's brought along for good measure. We wash them down with even more vodka and then both tuck into a can of cold rice pudding until it all takes effect.

And still, Apocalypse Now is looping.

```
[-They told me that you had gone
totally insane, and that your methods
were unsound.
-Are my methods unsound?
-I don't see any method at all, sir.]
```

'Why you only got one borr baby?' the Tom asks, knocking

back another vodka and refilling her glass.

I don't answer. I just cram rice pudding down my neck like an Ethiopian coming off detox. Why am I so damned hungry?

'It swollen; kina brack and brue,' she tells me with genuine concern. 'You need see doctor.'

I look between my legs. My nut sack is indeed a bloated mass of purple/black and completely numb. Maybe she's right.

Back to work and this time she means business, gobbling and mawing until we're at last starting to see the tent being pitched. Finally, I'm bucking like an epileptic bronco. She starts manoeuvring a condom into position, but I'm telling her.

'No, don't stop now. Do not fucking stop!'

I bury my head into a pillow, readying myself for a long overdue baby batter extravaganza when she suddenly stops.

A-fucking-gain.

'Nooo....' I scream at her, teetering on the edge of oblivion like Darth fucking Vader in Revenge of the Sith.

When I look up, she's got her attention focused on the door – at Henry [MONSTER COCK!] stood in the entrance still with his hand on the latch and staring at us wide-eyed.

```
[It smelled like slow death in there,
malaria, nightmares.]
```

*

It's 9:15am and we're sat in Henry's car. Henry and me on our way to work. Me still in his dressing gown, sweatpants and Crocs and holding the dregs of the vodka bottle.

As it turns out somewhere over the weekend I'd lost a day. It's Monday, I'm off my tits and the disciplinary hearing starts in less than an hour. Henry and me, we avoid any conversation, not that I'm capable of holding one anyway. He stares straight ahead with a tight, ten-to-two grip of the steering wheel, clean, sober and fresh from his weekend in the country with the kids. Me, I'm sweating and shivering and my heart rate is through the roof, but still, he refuses to close the window, unreasonable cunt that he is.

On the radio, dead Whitney is singing, so I turn up the volume and give her some ad-lib, out-of-tune backing vocals:

```
I believe that all children are the
future
Teach them all and see them lead our
way
Give them all our beauty they will
need inside
Show them a lots of pride and make it
easier..!
```

By the time the chorus comes around, I'm busting my lungs to reach the high notes and there are tears streaming down my face.

```
I realised long, long ago, never to
talk in anyone's shadows
If I fail, if I believe
At least I know that I succeed.. ed
No matter what they take away from me
They'll never take my dignity..

Because the bigges ..test love of
all..
```

'Carl,' shouts Henry above me and dead Whitney, not taking his eyes off the road. 'You seriously need to see someone.'

And I'm thinking, that's the second person to tell me that this morning.

'I already am Henry,' I shout back, toasting my psychiatrist and taking another slug of the vodka. 'I already am.'

25 ASSESSMENT TYPES

[Part of me was afraid of what I would find and what I would do when I got there. I knew the risks, or imagined I knew. But the thing I felt the most, much stronger than fear, was the desire to confront him]

The Chair, who is a man, browses his notes, says something to the person to his left, slips on a pair of glasses and looks around the boardroom table, and does a double take on me, still in Henry's dressing gown, sweatpants and Crocs. But someone has relieved me of the vodka bottle.

Fuckers.

'My name is Mr John Davies,' he says, almost wearily.

'I am the designated senior manger who will be chairing this hearing.'

He introduces the other two people making up the official

committee and handful of other observers representing the various factions of Carols, oestrogen fuelled, boiler mafia from in and around the college, relishing the prospect of my public defilement. Jeremy is here of course, as he is with all meetings, and Carol, who filed the initial complaints. I'd call it a kangaroo court but the obese woman from HR taking the minutes would make a mockery of the metaphor.

'For the record, this appeal hearing is for the summary dismissal of Mr Carl Waxman for Gross Misconduct on the grounds of..'

The Chair who is a man raises his glasses and squints at his notes.

'Er.. a multitude of offences laid out in your notes, any one of which would be grounds for summary dismissal, but collectively, the college felt made for a much stronger and frankly,' he actually sniggers at this point. 'Almost indefensible case. However, we will proceed.'

Tosser.

I glance down the list in front of me and close one eye to focus:

- Wilful refusal to comply with reasonable management instruction
- Deliberately falsifying records
- Using grossly offensive behaviour towards a member of staff
- Incapacity at work through an excess of drugs
- Using college equipment to access pornographic material during work time

- Deliberately causing damage to the college property
- Inappropriate relations with learners

You've got to hand it to Carol, she's been doing her homework, and I'm beginning to wonder whether turning up was worth even the effort I'd made. Not that I've made much. I tried to scrape enough coke together to fortify myself in the disabled toilets earlier with a small line, but my hand was shaking so much I dropped most of it down the pan which goes to prove Kilgore's hypothesis at least: Charlie don't even fucking float, let alone surf.

I had a brief argument with the Tom earlier which was resolved by Henry agreeing to give her the extra £20 I didn't have to pay for her services she didn't perform, before I necked more pills of indiscriminate nature and got into Henry's car.

The Chair, who is a man, goes on.

'Mr Waxman has stated the grounds of his appeal in writing, for which we should also all have a copy?'

I've appealed? I'm pretty sure I did no such thing. Murmurs of affirmation reverberate around the room.

'Can I also add that a decision will not be reached today. Recommendations by this committee will be passed to the Dean who will consider it at a further meeting, and a final decision will be made within the week.'

Carol stares at me tight lipped, on the one hand looking smug and confident, on the other angry and disgusted. I can't blame her. I look like I've contracted rabies or something. I swallow hard against the rising bile. Through the skylight I watch wisps of clouds rolling overhead, trying to find some Buddha room and praying for the merciful distraction of a seagull's feathery arse.

Immediately Carol stands up, attempting her territorial pissing routine.

'Mr Chair, I want to register an objection to these appeals, which are fundamentally just technicalities.'

The Chair, who is a man, raises a hand and interrupts her. He's having none of it.

'Ms Grese, you will have your chance to speak in due course, but please let us stick with procedure for now. Whatever your views, Mr Waxman does have a right to be heard. Now there is a lot to get through here, so, Mr Waxman would you please address the first allegation of...'

He raises his glasses again at the notes in front of him.

'Wilful refusal to comply with reasonable management instruction.'

I've got very little to say in my own defence except for a very insincere plea for clemency I managed to write on a postit in Henry's car, that I can't even bloody read now.

'Er..'

I feel sick. I need to piss. The bile is rising fast and I'm in in the early stages of a fucking panic attack here.

'Mr Chair, for the record, I will be Mr Waxman's appointed representative.'

All eyes turn on Jeremy with a look of surprise.

'Is this OK with you Mr Waxman?' the Chair, who is a man, asks.

Jeremy just nods at me and winks. I nod back.

'Very well, for the record Mr Jeremy Howard will be representing Mr Carl Waxman in this hearing.'

He makes sure the obese woman from estates has got that down before continuing.

'Now, Mr Howard, please outline Mr Waxman's appeal against the first charge, which I also believe relates in particular to assessment procedures taking us on to the second charge of deliberately falsifying documents.'

Jeremy taps a wad of paper on the table, stands up and reaches across to hand them to the Chair. He sits back down, clasps his hands together, composes himself then begins.

'Mr Chair, ladies and gentlemen. May I draw your attention to these memos in just one monthly period of Mr Waxman's employment, which alludes to these first two charges? They suggests a ratio of 30% teaching time to 70% extra curricular planning and assessment time. They then go on to impose further amendments to existing practices while compelling Mr Waxman to undertake several CPD courses and attend unscheduled meetings.'

The Chair, who is a man, passes the printouts to someone else, takes off his glasses and looks at Jeremy.

'At no point did Mr Waxman ever directly refuse to carry out any 'reasonable management instructions,' he was simply unable to keep up with the sheer volume of work imposed on him. According to my calculations Mr Chair, and assuming Mr Waxman is allowed the courtesy of having his weekends to pursue his own leisure interest.'

I can feel eyes, looking at me, imagining the kind of leisure interests I have.

'And taking into account his travel time, Mr Waxman would be working an estimated 18 hour day which would constitute working unreasonably long hours, for well below the minimum wage.'

'No-one works in teaching for the amazing remuneration Mr Howard,' says the Chair, who is a man, much to the amusement of his fellow committee members.

'Dismissing an employee for refusing to work physically and financially impossible hours would not sit well with an employment tribunal Mr Chair.'

And within a second the smiles of the committee are wiped.

'Alluding to the second charge of falsifying records,' continues Jeremy. 'This is due in no small part to Mr Waxman being forced to duplicate some assessment papers owing to very severe time constraints imposed on him by the very person who is now so vigorously pursuing his dismissal. I wouldn't be surprised if Mr Waxman isn't considering a charge of constructive dismissal against the college.'

Why didn't I think of that? Time convolutes and reconstitutes and I'm vaguely aware of someone talking to me again.

'..and grossly offensive behaviour toward a fellow tutor. Mr Waxman? Mr Waxman are you feeling OK?'

It takes a gargantuan effort to bring my eyes back to the horizontal and meet that of the Chair, who is a man. I nod again and open my mouth to say something, I'm not entirely sure what, but Jeremy stops me.

'As with most of these charges, it is simply a case of misunderstanding.' he tells the Chair, who is a man.

Carol stands up.

'Misunderstanding!? He can't wriggle out of this one, we have CCTV footage of that.. specimen sexually assaulting a female colleague in the corridor with - you know, his... his thingy sticking out!'

She points a shaking finger towards my offensive 'thingy.' I cover my groin and scowl at her.

'And we have the victim's full statement to back it up,' she adds.

The Chair, who is a man, waves his hand in the air irritably.

'Carol sit down please! You will have your turn.'

Carol sits back down reluctantly and Jeremy continues.

'Up until the time of the incident to which Ms Grese refers, Mr Waxman's academic results, records and popularity amongst the learners were a testament to his commitment to professionalism and the excellence to which this college aspires. In light of that, Mr Waxman's actions on that day were wholly out of character. The day the incident took place was his first day back after a brief stay in hospital because of.. a condition, for which he continues to receive treatment for and is still on prescribed medication.'

The Chair who is man again checks his notes.

'Yes,' he confirms. 'We have that on record. Please continue.'

'He is obviously mortified by his actions, but his behaviour that day resulted from a severe reaction to a cocktail of prescribed medication. Mr Waxman needed to use the disabled toilets for medical reasons. However, he was forced to use the stairs because of the colleges on-going issues pertaining to the accessibility lift. This further exasperating his painful condition, resulting in him overdosing on painkillers and other medication which caused an adverse reaction - directly contributing to the incident.'

The accessibility lift is a constant source of embarrassment to the college management and the committee squirm in their seats.

'As an aside, may I bring to the attention of the committee that the college has been repeatedly reprimanded for not making the required accessibility adjustments for disabled people.'

'It's not a matter of neglect or willing, Mr Howard,' protests the Chair who is a man. 'More a matter of budget.'

'A matter the college will not resolve by persecuting people with additional needs like Mr Waxman, who are forced to over medicate as a result of using alternative and inappropriate facilities, Mr Chair! In fact it may even be opening itself up to a class action law suit of unimaginable scale.'

Jeremy hands a piece of paper to the Chair who is beginning to look like an anxious man.

'This is a signed statement from a senior consultant at the hospital to which Mr Waxman continues to be an outpatient. It corroborates Mr Waxman's grounds for appeal on this charge, and confirms his medication has been changed to avoid any recurrence of these adverse reactions. You may keep that copy for your records.'

The Chair, who is a man, dips his glasses and glances at the paper.

'I'd just like to add Mr Chair, that the circumstances of the incident have been fully explained to the staff member in question and she is not interested in pursuing the matter any further.'

Not after I found the dirty slut in the toilets with Henry anyway.

'She has consented to counselling within college and I do not anticipate, in my professional opinion, her experiencing any lasting effect.'

The Chair, who seems to be a relieved man, looks up from the consultant's statement.

'Well that seems to be in order. Does this also explain the second charge of incapacity at work through an excess of drugs?'

'It does, Mr Chair.'

The Chair who is a reassured man, has a brief discussion with another committee member then looks up and asks.

'Does anyone have anything to add?'

Carol stands up, opens her mouth then sits back down, temples pulsing as she rifles through her notes for some crumb of repost. She obviously realises it must have all been a big 'misunderstanding.'

'Moving on then,' says the Chair, who is a satisfied man. 'How does Mr Waxman answer the charge of..'

Again he lowers his glasses.

'Using college equipment to access pornographic material during work time.'

Carol holds up her hand politely.

'Mr Chair, I have a list of Internet websites Mr Waxman has accessed during this term, given to me by the IT department and a printed copy of just some of the grotesque material he downloaded. May I hand them out?'

The bitch has actually got IT to access my account! She holds up a wad of paper. The Chair, who is a hesitant man, nods cautiously. Jeremy smiles indulgently at Carol and stands up again.

'Mr Waxman teaches a module commonly referred to as 'PhotoShopping,' in which blemishes, tattoos and unsightly pubic hair are digitally removed from lingerie and glamour models. It is an industry standard retouching procedure, and a vocational skill that stakeholders entering this particular field will need to understand. To dismiss Mr Waxman on this basis would be like dismissing a beauty therapist tutor for teaching a bikini waxing procedure.'

Carol, oblivious to the wry smiles appearing on committee's faces, carries on handing out the incriminating evidence; images of glamour models and porn stars, as Jeremy continues.

'It also emancipates female stakeholders by demystifying unrealistic notions of beauty, portrayed in the media. As you have undoubtedly heard, Mr Waxman was recently involved with the Brighton SlutWalk, which proves he is a tireless proponent of women's empowerment.'

Even some of Carol's attack dogs are looking doubtful now in the face of my obvious feminist credentials.

'Also may I point out that Mr Waxman's sessional and lesson plans can be found on the college intranet, for which his line managers have full access. If they had any misgivings over this module, they could have addressed it at any time.'

Carols technophobia is legendary, and she avoids the college intranet on pain of death. Jeremy holds up some printouts of his own.

'I too have a record of Internet access Mr Chair; a comprehensive history of every staff member in the Art, Design and Media Faculty.'

Suddenly Carol looks up.

'Almost all of Mr Waxman's site visits can be explained in terms of work related projects. The same, I suspect cannot be said of certain staff members who access for example..'

Jeremy puts on a pair of slim designer spectacles, which makes him look even more like a lawyer and pauses for full effect before reading from the list.

'Sperm donor sites, cat rescue sites, matchmaking and dating websites..'

A ripple of nervous laughter goes around the room as Jeremy reads on. Some are amused but most are making a mental note to delete their Internet history as soon as they get back.

'This is a disciplinary hearing for Mr Waxman!' Carol interrupts. 'This surely isn't the right forum for separate allegations Mr Chair?!'

Jeremy stops mid list and takes off his glasses.

'If Mr Waxman's Internet history can be brought to bear on this charge, surely in his defence he should at least be given the opportunity of a comparative analysis in relation to his peers and managers?'

The Chair who is a conflicted man, briefly discusses it with some of the other committee members.

'I think you have given a sufficient account in relation to this charge Mr Howard. Should we move on?'

Silence.

'Ms Grese, have you anything further to add?'

'No, Mr Chair,' says Carol, snatching back the few sheets

she's managed to hand out.

The Chair, who is a man back in control, reads the next charge.

'Deliberately causing damage to the college property. This relates to two charges, one of wilful damage to a printer, the other an accusation of putting 'bugs' on Ms Grese's computer.'

Jeremy holds up both hands.

'Well, Mr Waxman has no defence for this one, Mr Chair. In a moment of extreme agitation he admittedly tried to repair a printer himself, causing some internal damage for which he was never given the opportunity to compensate the college. But who here can say they have never become frustrated with a printer?'

A murmur of general empathy ripples around the room, particularly from the older members. One of the committee members who until now had remained stony faced and silent, begins an anecdote of how he once threw a printer from a bedroom window, which fans out into a general discussion on general printer vexation before the Chair, who is a man, bangs on the table, bringing the hearing back to order.

'Very well,' he says. 'And the charge of putting 'bugs' in Ms Grese's computer?'

Jeremy smiles like he's correcting the innocent assumptions of a child.

'Mr Chair, a 'bug' is a small annoying flaw in a machine, that we all experience from time to time, especially with printers.'

Playing to the floor now, Jeremy is slowly winning over the committee and the room, much to Carol's chagrin.

'Maybe you are referring to a computer 'virus?''

The Chair frowns then looks over to Carol.

'Ms Grese, would you like to rephrase your statement.'

Before Carol can say anything, Jeremy butts in.

'Mr Chair, I don't think it would be correct procedure to allow a witness statement to be altered mid hearing!'

Carol gets to her feet again.

'That bastard wrecked two of my computers! I lost weeks of work..'

'Ms Grese!' scolds the Chair, who is an assertive man, riding over her. 'Please control yourself or you will be asked to leave the room!'

Carol, her face flush red, glowers at the Chair. And you just know he'll be next on the feminazi hit list of undesirables.

'Mr Chair,' says Jeremy calmly. 'If we are talking about a 'virus', as I suspect we are, they are generally acquired by opening erroneous attachments on external emails, which, as we all know, is against college policy.'

Jeremy turns to look at Carol.

'Someone who is flouting college policy by accessing

external mail during college time and whose IT knowledge is, how can I put this? Less than the required minimum expected of staff in a modern college setting - can easily be fooled into opening these attachments. In doing so, they infect their OWN computer. Does the witness statement completely rule out this possibility?'

All eyes now turn to Carol who looks like she's in the throws of an internal seizure.

'Well what about this?!' she says, audibly stabbing at the last item on the agenda in front of her. 'What about these witness statements that say this monster is having.. liaisons with some of his female students?!'

'Stakeholders,' Jeremy calmly corrects her.

'Do I take it we're moving on to the next charge, Mr Chair?' asks Jeremy, matter-of-factly, and moving a sheet aside.

The Chair, who is man ready to go home, sighs.

'It would appear so,' he says, moving a sheet aside too.

'The fact is, they are children under our care!' screams Carol.

'Mr Chair, may I just defuse some of this inflammatory rhetoric for the record?' Jeremy says, sounding like a Zen master of calm, in the eye of a shit storm.

'These are not children in school; they are young adults - stakeholders, in the lifelong learning sector, and we are under an obligation to treat them as equals. To treat them in any other way would be negative differentiation. Furthermore, nowhere in the college code of practice does it say a consensual amorous relationship between a lecturer and stakeholder of legal age are grounds for summary dismissal. To prevent it may even be a violation of their human rights and subject to legal challenge. At no time was Mr Waxman made aware of any wrongdoing. He received no verbal or written warning..'

'I did Mr Chair!' interjects Carol. 'I gave him a verbal warning the morning before he attacked Hilary! I said to him..'

'You said to Mr Waxman.. and I quote,' interrupts Jeremy, teasing out a sheet of paper from his wad. 'Bastards like you, always slip up eventually. I'm gathering evidence on you and I'm going to see you up before a disciplinary hearing, I promise you!'

Jeremy places the paper on the desk and looks solemnly at the committee.

'Is this the type of verbal warning the committee would find admissible?'

'But this... this paedophile is preying on innocent...'

'MS GRESE!' shouts Jeremy. 'Your use of the word 'paedophile' has been duly minuted.'

He points at the HR woman in the corner tapping furiously at her laptop to catch up.

'I'm sure if Mr Waxman were a vindictive man, he would seek legal redress for such blatant defamation. The word you may possibly be looking for is ephebophilia - a preference for late pubescent youth - and it is certainly not grounds for dismissal. In my professional lifetime there have been great strides towards the understanding that people should not be marginalised or discriminated against because of what society deems as inappropriate desires or characteristics.'

He puts two balled up fists on the desk in front of him and scowls at Carol.

'It wasn't so long ago that minorities and homosexuals like myself were treated in a similar unenlightened fashion by bigots. I for one hope that in the very near future ephebophilia too, will be embraced by this college to make it a truly diverse and equal workplace we can all be proud of.'

Silence.

No one knows what the fuck he is banging about, but it sounds plausible enough. Jeremy draws a deep breath.

'Mr Chair, there are no conflicts of interest being brought to light here, nor any specific charges of harassment. Again, there are no grounds for dismissal on this final charge either. Mr Chair, perhaps I can be frank?'

The Chair, who is a spent man, takes off his glasses and rubs the bridge of his nose.

'Please do Mr Howard, please do.'

'I hesitate to bring this up for all of it's legal ramifications, but what we're witnessing here is institutionalised bullying of the worst kind, that could easily form the basis of a claim against the college for wrongful and/or constructive dismissal. Mr Waxman also has a strong case of discrimination under the Gender Recognition Act 2004,

The Human Rights Act 1998, The Criminal Justice Act 2003 and the Public Sector Duty Act 2010.'

'Discrimination, Mr Howard? How so?' asks the Chair, who is a man with enough indoctrination training to know that discrimination charges can only flow in one direction - towards straight white men; not from them.

Jeremy suddenly thrusts a statement in the air like he's Neville Chamberlain.

'I have in my hand, a statement from Mr Waxman's psychotherapist confirming a diagnosis of acute Gender Dysphoria!'

Silence. Again.

'What's.. gender dysphoria, Mr Howard?' asks the Chair, who hasn't been reading his Diagnostic and Statistical Manual of Mental Disorders - Fifth Edition, lately.

'Formerly known as gender identity disorder, Mr Chair.' says Jeremy, referring obviously to Diagnostic and Statistical Manual of Mental Disorders - Fourth Edition.

I'm wondering what the verb is for a collective jaw drop.

'Mr Waxman.. thinks he is a woman?!' asks the Chair who is now, a very alarmed man.

Jeremy slaps a hand on my shoulder, and is on the brink of tears.

'This poor woman, despite fighting her own personal demons, and having to hide her true nature for fear of discriminatory reprisals such as she is now experiencing, has put her heart and soul into this establishment and this is the thanks she gets. Bullying, discrimination, defamation and finally a dismissal on the grounds of vindictive conjecture. Not only is it shameful, it's highly illegal!'

He glances around the room, a towering figure of morality and righteousness, waving a copy of the Equality Act like some civil rights preacher.

'Now, the last thing she wants, is to see is the good name and reputation of this college, which she cherishes, dragged through the courts and media. But it seems she has been afforded no other option.'

The Chair, who is becoming an increasingly fearful man, coughs.

'Mr Howard, can I remind you that any recommendations by this committee can be taken to appeal by Mr.. er, Ms Waxman by due process. It may not even come to that. There's no need..'

'Mr Chair, for Ms Waxman, the damage is already done. She has been forcefully outed in a shameful display of public humiliation.'

Shame and humiliation is right. I've got three days of stubble and my hair hasn't seen a comb since the date with Rachel and my party with Colonel Kilgore the previous week. I wasn't aware that I'd turned into a woman in the process though. Although to be fair I'm off my tits on blow, coke, Oxycodones, Benzodiazepines, gin, vodka and a cocktail of alcoholic miniatures of indeterminate nature, so who knows what the hell I am anymore.

So it could be true.

I pull my sweatpants down to check my genital status. Disgusted gasps erupt from around the room. Even Carol is speechless for a change. The pudgy fingers of the obese woman from estates, hang over the keyboard like they're about to dive headlong into a party bag of minstrels.

Waiting.

Waiting.

'However,' says Jeremy, coughing and drawing the room's attention back to him. 'Perhaps the committee can recommend a private meeting between myself, as Ms Waxman's representative, and the Head Dean, that would help us salvage the situation in a manner that would be agreeable to all parties?'

'No!' shouts Carol, finding her voice again.

'Shut up woman!' says the Chair, who is finally a Chair-man.

Jeremy scowls at her too.

'If Ms Waxman wishes to pursue these defamation charges against you Ms Grese, his legal representative will contact you in due course. In the meantime may I council you on your highest discretion?!'

Ouch!

Silence.

Dead air.

[It might have been my mission, but it sure as shit was the Chief's boat.]

Through the glass door to the room I see uniformed officers in a heated discussion with the guys from Special Branch, perhaps the face of my psychiatrist too. For a split second - for an almost imperceptible moment, I think I even catch the face of Rachael's mother. From outside comes the voice of Muslim protest gathered by some twitter orchestrated flash mob.

It would seem the party has only just started.

I slowly stand and point a finger at the committee. I feel I should contribute something to proceedings; at least have some say in my personal defence. It's the only dignified thing to do.

Swaying slightly, my sweatpants hanging open I am possessed with the indignant wrath of Colonel Walter E Kurtz himself.

'As for the charges against me.' I slur, pausing to let the bile settle again. 'I am unconcerned. I am beyond their timid lying morality, and so I am beyond caring.'

Fucking Genius.

People would talk about my redemptive speech for years to come. A plaque would be raised and people with tears in their eyes, would bring flowers and talk about me in whispers.

Then I look at Jeremy and am struck with a lightening bolt epiphany. The bile quickly rising again I point at him and ask.

'Have you.. you been sending me flowers?!'

He looks away slightly and turns a shade of pink.

Then I explode a voluminous amount of vomit across the room. People dive out of the way as a second, then a third spectacular bout of regurgitated rice pudding arches across the tables and chairs, creating bedlam, before I pass out in a heap, pissing myself and proving beyond doubt that 'multi tasking' is not at all gender specific.

26 ASSESSMENT METHODS

[Sell the house. Sell the car. Sell the kids. Find someone else. Forget it. I'm never coming back.]

Three months later.

FAO: Hospital Administrator Broadmoor Hospital

Re: Mr Carl Waxman - Psychiatric Notes # 3

I examined the patient Carl Waxman once again, this time at Broadmoor for the purpose of psychiatric evaluation. I also drew on the material supplied to me by the police service, Special Branch (Counter Terrorism Division), social services and my previous psychiatric observations. There were also witness statement from the mother of the patient's former fiancé - Beverley Weiner - and the patient's partner - Jeremy Howard.

The patient arrived unconscious at A&E by ambulance following a collapse at work, with a drug and alcohol overdose and acute septicaemia. Witness statements allude to the fact he was extremely 'unkempt' and delusional. Toxicology reports confirmed a cocktail of drugs and alcohol.

He frequently laughed, cried and masturbated during psychiatric evaluation and seemed depressed, but I was unable to establish suicidal ideation. He was disorientated in all three spheres. His memory for immediate, recent and remote events was vague - his judgement poor. The patient was uncooperative during psychiatric evaluation, looking older than his stated age and responding to questions in delusional manner, claiming, 'I'm not presently disposed to discuss these operations, sir.'

Chief Complaint:

See previous report.

History of present illness:

See previous report.

Psychiatric History:

See previous report.

Medical History:

No record of any previous medical conditions.

Criminal History:

The patient has been arrested twice in the last six months for sexual assault and incitement to racial hatred (it should be noted that on his arrest for the latter, the patient was in fact, dressed as a woman - evidence transsexualism?). In the first instance the patient was released without charge and the second he received a police caution.

The mother of the alleged 'fiancé', while initially enthusiastic about pursuing a charge of rape, retracted the allegations on learning of the patient's injuries and mental state.

Mental Status Check:

The patient is disorientated with depression and has now developed symptoms of multi personality disorder. Apocalyptic delusions are presenting themselves in addition to the disorders outlined in the previous reports.

Precipitants:

The patient has locked himself into a perpetual cycle of self-harm and continues to develop a multitude of psychiatric disorders. He was under psychiatric observation but consistently missed sessions and did not respond well to the little treatment he received.

Cross-Sectional View of Current Cognitions and Behaviours:

In the most recent mental status examination the patient began displaying symptoms of multi personality disorder, taking on the persona of a 'Captain Wallace.' who appears to be an American soldier, living in close proximity to other males on a boat in Vietnam. (Perhaps homo-erotic in nature?). This 'Captain Wallace,' revealed a contradictory, imprecise religiosity that involved a preoccupation with a pagan figure known as 'Colonel Walter E Kurtz,' and an imminent 'apocalypse.' However, when pressed, he denied any knowledge of either, saying.

'I am unaware of any such activity or operation - nor would I be disposed to discuss such an operation if it did in fact exist.'

A further problematic situation is that, despite now having both testicles removed (the second due to advanced septicaemia), the patient is still unable to realise his true repressed sexuality because he is on testosterone replacement therapy and incarcerated with other males. I believe this has merely exacerbated the patient's alpha-male, pseudo-persona which is a major contributing factor to his rapidly declining mental health.

Diagnosis:

- Gender dysphoria. (NB referred to as 'gender identity disorder' in report # 1)
- Drug and alcohol abuse
- Mixed sexual deviation coupled with chronic masturbation.
- Multi personality disorder
- Apocalyptic delusions
- Depression

Prognosis:

Symptoms have become progressively worse and the latest incident, in my opinion was a final 'cry for help.' Given the circumstance that sexual reassignment surgery is already virtually complete, it is my opinion that the patient treatment should be accelerated. Testosterone replacement therapy should be withdrawn immediately and replaced with cross-sex hormone therapy. This would help the patient to feel more comfortable within himself/herself - both mentally and physically - and to begin the process of altering his/her body so that it is more in sync with his/her true gender identity. The patient should then acclimatise more readily to his/her repressed gender role. A combination of compulsory psychotherapy and behaviour modification therapy should be made available to back this up.

Conclusion:

This is a complex case. The patient consistently demonstrated an inability to appreciate and accept his primary diagnosis (gender dysphoria) or to conduct him/herself in a manner that is not a danger to him/herself or others. It is my firm belief that if he/she is returned to the community under his/her own care and further exposed to male-centric behavioural patterns, this condition will deteriorate. He/she will most certainly return to a pattern of severe self-harming. A witness statement from a Counter Terrorism Officer again alludes to the patient's continuing desire for cosmetic surgery and an identity change (full witness statement attached). In that respect I recommend the patient continue to be sectioned under the Mental Health Act 1983 for his/her own safety.

The patient's partner - Mr Jeremy Howard, has been a crucial part of his support network and supplying background information that the patient has been hitherto reluctant to divulge, particularly the patient's repressed homosexuality. Mr Howard has also coordinated legal action on behalf of the patient against his former employer and looks likely to win substantial damages for discrimination. Mr Howard intends to use this compensation to establish an Equality Consultancy partnership. I have given permission for Mr Howard to use the patient's case to be used for promotional purposes also, because I believe it will give the patient some excellent occupational focus. In that respect, Mr Howard should be given greater role and say in the patients vicissitude, which should aid longer term recovery and minimise the risk of relapse and/or re-hospitalisation.

In a final note, I would henceforth recommend that the patient be referred to, and addressed as female, to facilitate his acclimatisation to his imminent, agenda identity transition.

Catherine Cohen. BA (Hons), BABC

[She was close, real close. I couldn't see her yet, but I could feel her, as if the boat were being sucked upriver and the water was flowing back into the jungle.]

27 MAKING DECISIONS AND GIVING FEEDBACK

[Horror... Horror has a face... and you must make a friend of horror. Horror and moral terror are your friends.]

3 years later.

I'm thinking:

'Women are never stronger than when they arm themselves with their weaknesses.'

I wish I could take credit for it, but it's Madame Marie du Deffand. I'm trying to come up with our company's 'inspirational motto' for next month, but my head is literally all over the place today.

Yes, literally.

Whatever it is, it'll take a lot to beat last months:

'No-one is better than anyone else and everyone is the best at everything!'

Genius, I think you'll agree?

Jeanette, comes in with my appointment diary and a vase of fresh cut flowers which she arranges neatly on the window sill, all the while filling me in on the office gossip. She's such a chatterbox, but as efficient as a Swiss watch. I stir some Manuka honey into my chamomile tea and stroll to the window to help her. Blowing on the tea I gaze down at Joanna-public scurrying around Canary Wharf. Men and women in sharp suits, rushing to their offices with Starbucks and hot pastries in hands, looking frazzled and stressed.

Not in our office though.

Not today at least.

I've swapped my usual cropped pants, flats and floral top (maybe a blazer if I'm feeling stylish!) and instead wearing cranberry dungarees with a mustard sash. I know, I know, you don't have to be crazy to work here but it helps, right? And it's good to set an example, particularly when it comes to informality. The girls love it, and if nothing else it gives them something to gossip about at lunch.

The late comers - always the same culprits bless 'em - hurry into reception below and have obviously forgotten in their haste that it's 'dress down Friday.' I can see I'll be sending out yet another memo later, reminding them.

The quotation above reception reads:

'What the caterpillar calls the end, the rest of the world calls a butterfly.'

Lao-tzu wrote it, and it brings tears to my eyes every time I see it. It's a great ice-breaker with the overseas clients, particularly the Chinese.

We do a lot of consultancy work with offshoring operational franchises from Asia and the far East. They're never in the country for long, perhaps just enough to recruit our brightest and best before whisking those lucky soles off to foreign shores. But the time they are here, it's important they comply with our cultural safeguarding values, which is why they call on our services for help.

Overseas clients think our employment laws are a red tape nightmare, but our silk clad warriors joke about it being a gold-mine rather than a mine-field. They do love to party, and who can blame them? Their bonuses would make a hedge fund manager weep!

Svetlana and her business contacts have invested heavily in the sector – it's why she was so interested in Jeremy's equality expertise. She was certainly quick to spot that litigation was fast becoming the next economic bubble. It's certainly paying off.

Sadly her MEP fiancé died in a tragic accident with some electrical equipment, so she didn't marry in the end. Our personal relationship is very much on a business footing these days and strictly plutonic. I'm relieved that she no longer sees me as a sex object. I have skills and a brain, but above all I have feelings and special needs that she never really understood. By not appreciating my emotional needs, I feel she hurt herself more than me. I've tried recommending my psychotherapist to her but she isn't ready for the healing process yet and that's fine, we all move at our own pace.

But as the poster above my desk says:

'If you don't step forward, you're always in the same place.'

Down the corridor I see Jeremy, approaching. I see him because my office has an open door policy for all my employees. The name-plate on my desk says 'Go ahead, call me Carly' - you know, for that extra informal touch. But despite that, rarely does anyone pop by.

Go figure.

Listen to me, 'employees.' Jeanette will be making me put another 50p in the pot for that one later! What I mean to say is 'colleagues.' We frown on hierarchy here at Equalitas because everyone is of equal value.

The bullet points you should be making on Jeanette are:

- She is a Scorpio
- She is a kind, sensitive and a very spiritual person
- She always has time to listen to your problems

I really don't know how I coped before she came along. HR really outdid themselves in finding her. She's delightful, but can be a little scary at times. It's all..

'Carly, you'll be late AGAIN if you don't get a move on!'

And she's doing it again.

Tapping a finger at the open page of my appointment diary,

she asks, 'I hope you haven't forgotten about your interview with Jane Garvey this morning?'

Would you just listen to that? Jane Garvey interviewing little old me like I'm the new Martha Stewart or Oprah Winfrey. Honestly, who'd be interested in what I've got to say, really? And yes, I had forgotten about the interview if the truth be told.

It's then I realise I forgot to plug the Prius into the pod this morning when I arrived at the office.

'Jeanette, get security to charge my car immediately or I'll never make it to Salford in time!' I tell her, all of a fluster.

'Carly!' she says shaking her head with that look of dismay. 'Calm down, you don't have to drive! It's a telephone interview silly. The BBC don't seriously expect people to go up North! Besides, the interview starts in twenty minutes. Honestly, you're such a scatterbrain!'

We both laugh. Honestly, I would literally forget my head if it wasn't screwed on.

Yes, literally.

We do have a laugh Jeanette and me, because she's more than my PA, she's my friend. A good, close friend.

'Well get them to plug it in anyway or it'll have a flat battery!' I tell her.

'Don't worry about your precious car,' she scolds. 'I'll sort it!'

She's on to it immediately then we watch from the window

as one of the security guards - obviously not used to electric cars, struggles with the unfamiliar connection. She sighs and shakes her head.

'Honestly men; you'd think he'd know how to plug in a cable at his age.'

She does bunny fingers around 'plug in a cable,' and that's it. We're both bent over, hysterical with laughter.

'You can't say that Jeanette, it's sexist!' I tell her, dabbing at the underside of my eyes with a finger in a wholly futile attempt to stop the mascara running.

'It's not 'sexist' Carly,' she tells me assuredly. 'It's stereotyping. There's a difference.'

Jeremy is always accusing me of being too familiar with our 'colleagues' but I tell him straight.

'If friendship is my weakest point Jeremy, then shoot me, because that makes me the strongest person in the world!'

Talking of Jeremy, he's in my office now, arranging some notes at my desk. He barely notices me these days, and when he does he doesn't look at me the way he used to. He doesn't call me 'inspirational' or complement me on my clothes anymore and the flowers these days come on a company account. It's just another thing I'm processing with my psychiatrist. She tells me.

'Feeling valued is important Carly and you need to confront him about his passive aggressive behaviour!'

But I tell her.

'If he can't see how I feel, I shouldn't have to tell him!'

Maybe I'll send a memo out later reminding colleagues that hurting or insulting someone is not just mean and cruel but very much against the law. They don't really need reminding. After all who hasn't had a marketing call from Equalitas asking:

'Have your feelings been hurt or have you felt insulted or undervalued by your employer? Do you have low self-esteem? Then Equalitas can help you claim compensation on a no win no fee basis!'

More often than not we settle out of court, and make sure that part of that settlement involves one of our executive Equalitas e-learning, training packages with a full range of equality and diversity auxiliary services. Equalitas is a consultancy that motivates organisations and removes obstructive negativity in the workplace. Maybe that right there is next month's moto!

'Motivating Organisations & Removing Obstructive Negativity In Corporations'

Granted it's a bit longwinded, but it sends the right message I think. Maybe I'll start a new thread on that one to see how my colleagues feel about it.

Jeanette passes me the appointment diary, and oh, you should see that diary! Aside from the meetings, it's full of motivational speaking, women's awards, female scholarship fundraiser and book signings.

Did I mention the book? Well, as part of my post-op therapy I was encouraged to write about my feelings, then a ghost-writer friend of Jeremy's turned his magical editorial talents to it and before you could say chic-lit, it was in print!

'Changing Our Ways: Spiritual Healing & Intelligent Thinking.' is based around the real-life sessions with my wonderful psychiatrist and the pressures today's patriarchal society places on women. It's a kind of self help book full of the things women are just too afraid to discuss. I really don't think there are enough books about the pain and injustices women endure, or enough writing awards to recognise them.

At first they refused my entry onto the Guardian's Women Prize for Fiction, because technically they said, I wasn't a 'real woman'. Well that got Jeremy going didn't it? He told them straight.

'It's fine to exclude a man from a prize that brings prize money, free promotion and increased book sales, because that's equality, but to exclude a transgender transitionalist like Carly, well, that right there is discrimination, plain and simple!'

So my book was long-listed not only for the Guardian prize, but also a 'Bessie'. That's the BWPFF (Baileys Women's Prize for Fiction), as if anyone needs reminding, which celebrates excellence, originality and above all accessibility in women's writing. It never made it to the short lists, but that's hardly surprising, as there's some amazingly talented women writers out there, I'm really not in their league. However it received some lovely comments on the Mumsnet book club forum from people who thanked me for the 'amazing sharing'.

I don't want to make a big thing about being left off the shortlist, and I really don't blame the judges, they're all busy women after all and they have an ocean of women writers to get through. But sometimes they probably miss the subtleties that other, more feminine women can pick up on. I really don't mind. Really. My psychiatrist, whom I still see twice a week is helping me process rejection.

And get this.

She's only gone and qualified as a pan-denominational, spiritual healer and life coach too! So although she now charges double for her services, she's a 'three for two,' bargain for the NHS really. Despite being wealthy, I don't really see the need to go private when the NHS is such good value.

Jeanette leaves the office so I sit back at the desk and nibble a diet, chocolate rice cake to wash down my herbal photoestrogens.

'I don't want to come across as a victim or a monster in this interview with Jane Garvey.' I tell Jeremy as he sits across from me making last minute revisions to his flashcards. 'I want to come across as a survivor.'

Jeremy just looks at his watch and crosses his arms. When the call comes through from the BBC he talks briefly with the Woman's Hour producer before passing the call over to me. Apart from being the co-director of Equalitas, Jeremy is also my literary agent. And now he's a fully qualified lawyer, I tend to leave all the technical details in his capable hands. I'm more.. well I'm more of a 'people' person really.

Normally he would spend hours obsessing over editorial control, but he's more relaxed with the BBC, because as he tells me, their raison d'être is to promote a liberal manifesto, not challenge it.

I'm on!

According to Jane Garvey, she's read my book and she understands my pain. She sympathises with the heart-breaking ordeal and my humiliating victimisation. Me being a woman in pain and humiliated.

And a victim.

It's heart-breaking she tells me.

Jeremy and me, both of us wearing our wireless headsets; Jeremy now with his boom microphone turned off and holding up one of his flashcards that says:

'Featuring on the Women's Hour Power Game Changer List will raise my profile and give me the opportunity to show what an independent woman can achieve, despite the obstacles put in her way by an unequal and patriarchal society.'

Jane Garvey asks me how I feel about being shortlisted for Business Woman of the Year.

'I have a saying,' Jeremy's flashcard claims. 'Give 110 per cent and you will succeed. Fact. Setting up Equalitas - which incidentally provides unparalleled equality and diversity services to the public and private sector - was just the medicine I needed to restart my new life.'

Jane quickly tells her listeners that a range of equality and diversity services are available from other suppliers too. But these have men in charge so she doesn't mention them by name.

Moving on and talking of business, Jane wants to know if

I'm hurt by the 'groundless claims from certain quarters' that Equalitas's relentless pursuit of institutional sexism is at least partially responsible for the accelerating business exodus to the far east. Do I agree that we are somewhat to blame for Britain's decline in a range of international league tables. Jeremy quickly flicks through his colour co-ordinated flash cards, and holds one up.

'We're merely helping companies comply with the law; laws that persistent pressure groups have fought hard to force onto the statute books,' says the card, perhaps a little too grandiosely.

'That's democracy Jane, and besides, success is not about educational league tables or being economically competitive, it's about doing the very best you can, given your own individual circumstances. That's as true for countries as it is for people. We're all different, but we're all special in our own, individual way.'

Jane couldn't agree more, although I'm wondering whether Jeremy's cards are just a wee bit preachy.

'It's all in my book,' says another flash card. 'Changing Our Ways: Spiritual Healing & Intelligent Thinking - by Equalitas Press.'

And what's next for me, Jane wants to know; where do I go from here? So I tell her.

'I have another book coming out Jane,' which the flashcard tells me, 'aimed at the educational sector, 'Bringing Responsibility And Individual Needs to Differentiation, Equality And Diversity.'

Feeling more relaxed now and taking a sip of tea, the flash

card reminds me to tell her:

'Also by Equalitas Press - the fastest growing brand in publishing.'

Jeremy flips up another card, which is becoming vaguely irritating now.

'The Minister for Women and Equalities and I are also working on an education white paper: 'Change, Revolution And Progress,' because we both feel we should begin with the young.'

Going slightly off script now for a more personal touch I tell her:

'In the words of my personal hero, Nelson Mandela Jane, 'Whoever has the youth, has the future.'

Jane couldn't agree more. Jeremy not really understanding the close bond and friendship growing between us, *facepalms* himself and stabs a finger at the cards. Stick to the script! Honestly, lawyers, so controlling; so serious!

'We also chatted about some ideas for future legislation,' I tell her:

- Everyone's job to be declared 'of equal value'
- Injury to feelings' compensation to be increased for women, who are more sensitive than men
- Spiritual / homeopathic healing and back rubs to be made available on the NHS
- All cats to be included in the European Convention on Human Rights
- Women only shortlists for boardroom jobs and ministerial positions to be extended

- Increased, ring-fenced government grants to create even more opportunities for women
- Sex to be considered rape unless preceded by written consent
- Sexualisation of the female form to be declared a criminal offence - if perpetrated by a man
- Expand the number of women-only literary prizes

[This is the way the fucking world ends. Look at this fucking shit we're in, man. Not with a bang, but with a whimper. And with a whimper, I'm fucking splitting, Jack.]

###

ABOUT THE AUTHOR

Phil is currently a builder, who does some writing.

Living in Brighton, England, 'Kill All Men' is his first published novel, but the highlight of his career to date, is a beautiful patio he laid last year, which you could literally play snooker on.

Yes literally

He has had many jobs including heavy metal drummer, whale poo collector (Indian Ocean), yachtsman, computer games artist and graphics lecturer – a public sector job that was the inspiration behind, 'Kill All Men.'

Suddenly finding himself with three children, Phil is now planning a solo circumnavigation of the world, a trip which he anticipates will take several years.

In the meantime if you need a patio laid, call Phil for a competitive quote, because the writing sure as hell isn't paying the bills.

Printed in Great Britain
by Amazon.co.uk, Ltd.,
Marston Gate.